16<u>95</u>

The Investor's Equation:

Creating Wealth Through Undervalued Stocks

William M. Bowen IV
Frank P. Ganucheau III

Probus Publishing Company • 118 North Clinton • Chicago, Illinois 60606

This publication is designed to provide accurate and authoritative information in regard to the subject matter covered. It is sold with the understanding that the publisher is not engaged in rendering legal, accounting or other professional service. If legal advice or other expert assistance is required, the services of a competent professional person should be sought.

FROM A DECLARATION OF PRINCIPLES JOINTLY ADOPTED BY A COMMITTEE OF THE AMERICAN BAR ASSOCIATION AND A COMMITTEE OF PUBLISHERS.

Library of Congress Cataloging in Publication Data

Bowen, William M.
  The investor's equation.

  Bibliography:p.
  Includes index.
  1. Investments— Handbooks, manuals, etc. I. Ganucheau, Frank P.
II. Title. III. Title: Undervalued stocks.
HG4527.B64 1985   332.63'22   84-60950

ISBN 0-917253-00-0

Library of Congress Catalog Card No. 84:60950

Printed in the United States of America

1 2 3 4 5 6 7 8 9 0

To our greatest blessings,
Nancy and Betty

Contents

Preface

This book is about making money in the stock market. Although numerous books have been written on this subject, none take quite the approach the authors advocate. Instead of focusing on forecasting the price movement of various stocks, this book provides a method to measure the cheapness and the quality of a particular investment. The stockholder following this approach will come to think of himself as a part owner and investor in the corporation rather than a market player or speculator.

The authors met over six years ago; one of them was a broker and the other a portfolio manager. Early in their relationship they discovered a mutual interest, that being investing money based on definable and measurable value. They both also shared the desire to someday write a book that any serious investor could use to build a workable investment program. What the reader has before him is the result of five years of searching and studying to find the "truth" regarding financial investing. We define "truth" to be "that which if followed works."

We would like to recognize Benjamin Graham, Warren Buffett, David Dreman and Bill Ruane for their valuable contributions to the school of value investing. Any serious student on this subject would find his knowledge deficient if he did not read everything written by and about any one of these investors. The recommended reading list included in the appendix provides more information regarding these people. There are many other investors and researchers we studied, and we apologize to those we had to exclude from this list; however, most of them will be mentioned in the bibliography.

In preparing a manuscript of this nature, many people and relationships come into play. While we can't specifically thank everyone who helped us along the way, we would like to thank William M. Bowen III for his influence in being methodical and patient regarding financial matters, Frank Ganucheau Jr. for his guidance in viewing the economic world realistically and conservatively, the other members of our families for their encouragement and support, Ed Stocker for his guidance and encouragement, Michael Jeffers for his patience and help in getting this into the final product, and Robert L. Hagin for his assistance in locating a publisher.

In addition to those mentioned above, we would like to thank the good Lord for giving us the relationship and knowledge to produce what follows. If our message converts a few struggling market participants into true investors, we will have accomplished the mission we embarked upon.

Acknowledgments

Grateful acknowledgment is made to the following for permission to reprint previously published material:

CBS College Publishing: Adaptation of an excerpt from *Investment Analysis & Portfolio Management,* by Frank K. Reilly. Copyright 1979 by The Dryden Press, a division of Holt, Rinehart and Winston, pp. 163-165. Reprinted by permission.

Financial Management Association: "The Information Content of Price-Earnings Ratios," by Sanjoy Basu, pp. 53-63, reprinted by permission.

Fortune Magazine: "Gauging the Market's Prospects," by Mary Greenebaum, *Fortune,* January 10, 1983 issue, Vol. 107, No. 1, p. 97. Copyright 1983, Time, Inc., reprinted by permission of *Fortune.* All rights reserved.

Harper & Row, Publishers, Inc.: Specified excerpts and tables from *The Intelligent Investor,* 1959 ed., by Benjamin Graham, copyright 1949, 1954, 1959; and adapted excerpts in *The Intelligent Investor,* 4th rev. ed., by Benjamin Graham, copyright 1973, reprinted by permission.

Richard D. Irwin, Inc.: Summarized excerpts, "Evolution of Modern Portfolio Theory," by William F. Sharpe in *CFA Readings in Financial Analysis,* 5th ed., 1981; and chart and text, *Financial Statement Analysis: Theory, Application, and Interpretation,* by Leopold A. Bernstein, rev. ed., 1978; and excerpts, *The Stock Market: Theories and Evidence,* by Lorie and Hamilton, 1973, reprinted by permission of Richard D. Irwin, Inc.

Kidder, Peabody & Co.: Excerpts, "Excess Cash Flow Analysis—A New Approach to Determining Real Earnings, Dividend Sustainability, and Long-Term Growth of Corporations in an Era of Inflation," by Barre W. Littel, May 6, 1975; and tables and excerpts, "Financial Quality Profile—Introduciton to FQP Theory, Ratios and Scoring," by Barre W. Littel and Robert Levine, December 19, 1980, reprinted by permission.

Macmillan Publishing Company: Excerpts, *Competitive Strategy: Techniques for Analyzing Industries and Competitors,* by Michael E. Porter. Copyright 1980 by the Free Press, a division of Macmillan Publishing Company Inc., reprinted by permission.

The MIT Press: Excerpts, *An Introduction to Risk and Return from Common Stocks,* by Richard Brealy. Copyright 1969. Reprinted with permission. All rights reserved.

Prentice-Hall Inc.: Excerpts, *Inside the Yield Book,* by Sidney Homer and Martin L. Leibowitz, copyright 1972, Prentice-Hall Inc., Englewood Cliffs, NJ, reprinted by permission.

Moody's Investors Services, Inc.: Table, "Moody's Bond Record," Vol. 51, No. 3, p. 249, March 1984, New York, reprinted by permission.

Random House, Inc.: Tables and excerpts, *Contrarian Investment Strategy,* by David Dreman. Copyright 1979 by David Dreman, reprinted by permission of Random House, Inc.

Salomon Brothers, Inc.: "Financial Assets—Return to Favor," by R. S. Salomon, June 10, 1983, reprinted by permission of Salomon Brothers, Inc.

Standard & Poor's Compustat Services, Inc.: Tables, *Financial Dynamics Industrials,* "Annual Financial Analysis," 1982, reprinted by permission.

Value Line, Inc.: Tables, Value Line Investment Survey, "Selections and Opinions," *Value Line 900 Industrial Composite,* July 1978, 1983, reprinted by permission of Value Line, Inc.

Warren, Gorham & Lamont Inc.: "Market Inefficiencies: Opportunities for Profits," reprinted by permission of the *Journal of Accounting and Finance,* Spring, 1981, copyright 1981, Warren, Gorham & Lamont, Inc. All rights reserved.

CHAPTER I

Looking for an Investment Philosophy that Works

Have you called your broker in the height of a bull market only to find out your high-tech stock has become a low-tech performer? Whether you're the professional investor in search of a time proven investment philosophy or the serious amateur investor trying to create a successful investment program, this book will show you how to prosper from financial assets. It does not present a get-rich-quick scheme. Rather it presents an investment technique based on sound business logic and definable value.

As professional money managers, we often counsel people about the best methods and vehicles for accumulating and preserving wealth. Although at first glance this may not seem to be too difficult a task, you should note that one of the Rothschilds is said to have observed that, if he could be sure of transmitting to heirs a quarter of his capital, he would settle for that.

Rothschild probably didn't make it. The Rothschilds' business interests are no longer significant on a world scale. What remains are such frivolities as art collections, racing stables, and the wine chateaux.[1] In time, the ravages of taxation and inflation attack the returns on capital so that obtaining an incremental real return is extremely difficult. As a consequence, people seek advice. This is what investment counseling and money management are all about.

We have observed that people place confidence in those who have the strongest and most logical convictions about the future. How often is the question asked, "Where do you think the market is headed?"; or "Where do you think this stock is headed?" This kind of query is applicable not only to financial markets but also to the economy, to politics, to sports—virtually every activity in which people are engaged.

The next time something unfavorable happens in the Middle East or to the economy, notice how many people either offer a forecast of what the final outcome will be or ask what will happen next. When critical decisions have to be made, it seems the more concentrated the effort is that goes into forecasting the future, the more qualified are the forecasters who are relied upon.

An anecdote about people wanting to believe in a forecast of the future is based on an event in London in early 1524. This was a city awaiting its doom. Crowds of people gathered to listen to astrologers and soothsayers who all forecast the same thing. They predicted that, on February 1, the Thames would suddenly rise from its banks, engulf the city, and sweep away all the homes. The vision was described in detail to larger and larger groups of people. The forecast had started six months earlier when only a few soothsayers began to voice the prophecy. The word spread quickly. Month after month the warnings were repeated, and, as time passed, they became accepted with total assurance, although the Thames had always been the tamest of rivers.

At first, only a handful of families began to leave the city. But, as time passed, people left in increasing numbers. By mid-January, two weeks before the prophesied event, over twenty thousand people had evacuated London, including laborers, clergy, and noblemen.

When the day arrived for the river to leave its banks, some people did stay behind. It was even predicted that the river would rise slowly, allowing some who were quick enough to escape. When the fateful hour finally arrived, nothing happened. The river's tide ebbed and flowed, and it became apparent to the people that nothing unusual was going to happen. Still, just to be sure, most stayed away one more night. The next morning, with the river still within its banks, the crowds returned to the empty city, asking what had gone wrong. The soothsayers, to appease the crowds, said that they were indeed correct, that London was doomed, but that it would be in 1624, not 1524. They claimed to have made an error in their calculations.[2]

People have always been concerned with the future and with those who forecast it. The story demonstrates how certain groups in society can be seen as having extraordinary powers or insights and how these groups can lead and sway others in their thinking. The more credentials or qualifications a person has, the more he or she is apt to influence other people's thinking and to make them believe their forecasts. One must wonder if this is a result of the forecaster's charm and logic or of the listener's desire to believe in someone's forecast. We believe it is often a combination of both. We also feel, however, that most people very much want to believe that someone can predict the future. Why? Because one way to reduce uncertainties about today's decisions, whose results will be experienced in the future, is by believing that someone can tell you what's going to happen. When things don't work out quite as intended, the unforeseen variables can always be blamed. In fact, statistical studies have shown that the more uncertain the future, the more people rely on the "expert."

Does one really believe the future can be forecast? Does someone really know who will be the next president, what the price of oil will be six months from now, or what the deficit will be in 1985? Although trends can be identified, will they continue?

As money managers, we recognize that many of the conventional methods of doing things in our industry, over the past twenty years, have been based on forecasting. Also, we have observed the consistently poor performance of the average money manager and have questioned the traditional methods of investing. This book is a product of several years of study about the basic tenets of the industry, their failure, and, finally, about those investors who are successful.

Several money managers have demonstrated a knack for achieving above-average rates of return. Common points in their methods were observed and reasons for their success noted. What has emerged is a practical investment philosophy based on sound business principles that stand the test of time.

Our research for a successful investment philosophy began with a review of the results achieved by professional money managers as a collectivity. After all, this was the group to which more and more individuals turned in the late 1960s and again in the early 1980s to achieve the superior investment performance they couldn't get by themselves. A cadre of mutual fund salesmen convinced the public that these professionals were trained in the art of successful investing and spent most of their working time in that pursuit.

Charles Ellis in his article, "The Loser's Game," states that "The investment management business is built upon a simple, fundamental belief: Professional money managers can beat the market. That premise appears to be false."[3]

If that premise were accepted, it doesn't appear to be too difficult to find an approach to beat the market, which is a passive institution represented by the Standard & Poor's 500 Index. All a fund manager has to do is assemble a group of smart analysts and strategists who will supply the correct economic, industry, and company forecasts. Then he will buy only those companies that will do better than the Standard & Poor's averages. By looking at the results supplied by *Pensions & Investment Age* in their February 20, 1984, issue, however, the investor can see that, on the average, professional money managers don't beat the market.[4]

Table 1-1. Results: Money managers don't beat the market.

	Latest Year	Latest 3 Years	Latest 5 Years	Latest 10 Years
Standard & Poor's 500	22.6	12.3	17.4	10.7
Top performer	51.8	33.1	38.7	23.8
1st quartile	22.6	15.5	19.5	11.7
Median	18.8	12.7	17.1	9.9
3rd quartile	14.9	9.7	15.3	8.5
Lowest	.4	− 4.8	6.7	4.9

Note: All periods end December 31, 1983, and all figures are annualized total returns.

Source: "Firms Turn to Basics." (See references.)

For the most recent year (1983), only the top 25% of the stock funds in their survey performed better than the market as measured by the Standard & Poor's 500 Index. For the three-year period, just slightly more than half the managers beat the market, while for the five- and ten-year periods, fewer than half the managers reported returns better than the market averages. Obviously, the performance numbers can vary depending on the years included in the survey and the number of years measured. In any one given year, a money manager may do either very well or very poorly, which would not be representative of his long-term capabilities. That's why it is best to consider performance numbers over a three-year, five-year, and ten-year time span.

The authors hold that, to be considered successful, a money manager or individual must earn a rate of return on funds under their management higher than (1) the risk-free rate of return as measured by the performance of a short-term Treasury investment; (2) municipal securities for an investor subject to taxes; and (3) the Standard & Poor's 500 averages.

If, over the long run, these measurements are not achieved, the investor has not been compensated for the risk assumed by choosing individual holdings. We also argue that, over a relatively short period of time, it is possible to underperform these measurements.

Over several years, however, the performance should be expected to exceed these measurements on a cumulative basis. Why, then, have the majority of the managers failed to achieve returns better than these measurements? A look at the philosophies used by most money managers will offer some insights about their weaknesses.

Although these investment styles will be familiar to most professional investors, the nonprofessional person will find these brief discussions helpful in learning more about professional money management. Most likely, when an individual interacts with his broker, the brokerage firm has formulated its buy-and-sell recommendations based on one or a combination of these philosophies. Through understanding how professional analysts formulate their recommendations, and considering the biases in their philosophies, both the professional and nonprofessional investor can use Wall Street research more constructively.

Technical analysis

The first philosophy to be examined is called "technical analysis." To the uninformed, this label might imply a discipline that is very scientific, complicated, and exacting. In the investment business, however, the term "technical analysis" refers to charting or other timing measurements. The basic premise of this approach is that the past behavior of stock prices and trading volume can be used to forecast future movements in stock prices. The discipline studies only the price behavior of the stock, not the financial or economic fundamentals of the company.

The technical analyst believes that the price of a stock depends on supply and demand in the marketplace. The price has little relationship to value, if any such concept exists. Price is governed by psychological input of such volume and complexity that no one person can hope to understand and measure it correctly. Some technicians refuse to look at any economic or financial data for fear that it may distort their readings of the chart patterns.

"Technical analysis" is applied both to the market as a whole and to individual stocks. The fundamental principles apply to each. The assumption is that the market or particular stocks under scrutiny move in trends and will continue to move in those trends until there is contrary information or an indication of a change. Also past performance can be used to predict future performance. With his various tools, the technician attempts to gauge correctly changes in price trends and take advantage of these changes.

Technicians have many tools available such as bar charts, point and figure charts, volume figures, and dollar-flow studies—services that combine price behavior and volume to produce an indicator. With all these indicators at his disposal, the chartist makes a forecast of the future. Then, based on this forecast, he commits funds to various stocks.

Some technicians specialize in forecasting the market; others specialize in forecasting individual stocks; most specialize in both. The real performance comes in, first, timing the market to determine if an investor should be in stocks or cash reserves; and, second, selecting those stocks that will outperform the market. If this combination of market timing and stock selection can be achieved, the results can be spectacular. Here lies the attraction and challenge of being a market timer.

Although the allure and challenge attract many followers to this practice, the results achieved by technicians have been mediocre at best. Joseph Granville, a technician with many followers, gave a famous sell signal for the market in Janaury 1981. Granville appeared to have the key to the market when, in March 1980, he gave a buy signal, and the market advanced for about nine months. Then, in January 1981, he gave a sell signal, and the market initially went down on very heavy volume. After the initial pullback, the market firmed and actually went on to new highs until late in the spring of 1981. By June 1981, interest rates were at all-time highs, the economy was weakening, and the stock market began a slide that would keep it in the doldrums for over a year. Some market followers began to believe that once again Granville was correct.

In August 1982, when several Wall Street economists became positive on interest rates, the stock market followed the lead of the bond market and began one of the strongest rallies in financial history. Granville reiterated his sell signal and continued to stay bearish. The market performed spectacularly, rising from a low of 106 to a high of 134 as measured by the Standard & Poor's 500 Index. This, in about six weeks, is a 26.4% move. The Dow Jones was even more dramatic.

In our opinion, any time one misses a move of this magnitude, his system has failed. As one Wall Street observer aptly stated many years ago, "When someone finds a key to the market, it is not long until someone changes the lock."

Other stories abound about technicians with less notoriety than Granville's that can also offer evidence of the long-run failure of applying systems to the market.

The best conclusion can be drawn from John Train's *The Money Masters*. After interviewing and examining the experience of many successful investors who have consistently superior returns over long periods, Train did not find one of them who was either a technician or a market timer.[5]

The academic community has presented numerous studies over the past several years concerning the performance potential of using "technical analysis." Early studies centered on the random movements of stock prices and on how future stock prices were independent of previous prices.

One such study was done by Eugene Fama in 1965 as his doctoral dissertation. At intervals, he analyzed the prices and price movements of the 30 stocks in the Dow Jones Industrial Average. The intervals were one day and two weeks for over five years. The results and observations from his tests supported the "random walk hypothesis." If price movements are random, then, no matter what price and volume information one has or how he interprets a chart, this information is meaningless as a predictive instrument. The next price is entirely independent of the preceding one. Even if the price of a stock has risen seven days in a row, there is no guarantee what the price will be on the eighth day. It is actually a game of independent probability, just like flipping coins.

The academicians have also shown through computer studies that stock price changes are independent of previous prices. The "random walk hypothesis" states that past price and volume statistics by themselves contain no information that will allow the investor to get results better than those he would achieve by simply buying and holding securities. This theory leads to the conclusion that "technical analysis" is worthless as a forecasting tool.[6]

William Sharpe, a leading proponent of the Efficient Market Hypothesis and Modern Portfolio Theory (a subject to be discussed next), in another study tried to discover if market timing has value in the investment process. Sharpe concluded that a money manager who tries to time the market must be right three out of four times—after commissions and advisory costs—to make the effort begin to pay off. Studies show that the percentage of managers achieving these results is not very high.[7] Those on the top one year are on the bottom the next.

Another frequently used technical tool is "relative strength analysis." This technique is used for selecting individual stocks within the market that should outperform the market as a whole. Various chart services plot the relative strength of a stock to show that a stock is advancing more rapidly than a market advance or declining less rapidly than a market decline. The movement is graphically shown as a line that represents the stock's performance plotted against the market, or base line. If the stock line is pulling away from the market line, and some say that increasing volume is needed, then the stock is outperforming the market.[8]

Those who use "relative strength analysis" believe that, if the stock line crosses over the base line on increasing volume, the stock should be purchased, since

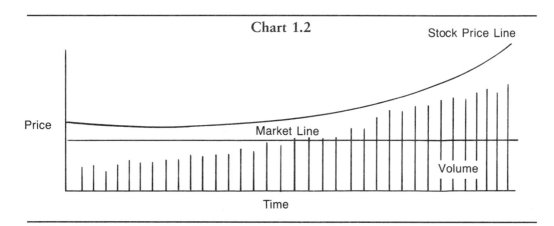

Chart 1.2

Stock Price Line

Price

Market Line

Volume

Time

the stock is being purchased by others and will go higher. This method of "technical analysis" faces the same acid tests as pure charting. The "random walk" research proves that future stock prices can't be determined by previous price behavior. Moreover, the authors' observation is that, in a declining market, this philosophy will have an investor rotate from groups that are already depressed into groups that are about to experience selling. When he seeks strength, he may be getting set for the next group to be liquidated. In weak markets, most selling rotates from one industry to another.

Ben Graham may have put it best when discussing "technical analysis." It is a philosophy that involves buying something because it has risen in price and selling something because it has declined in price. This is the reverse of sound business logic and is destined to fail as an investment philosophy.[9]

Efficient markets and modern portfolio theory

The second school of thought we will explore in investment management is the "efficient capital markets theory." An efficient market is one in which security prices adjust rapidly to the introduction of new information. It is believed that current security prices fully reflect all available information, including the risk involved.

The first assumption regarding efficient markets is that a large number of participants exist who are trying to maximize their returns. These participants are constantly analyzing their securities and are acting independently of each other.

The second assumption is that information comes to the markets in a random manner, and that news or events over a period are independent occurrences.

The third assumption is that persons adjust their holdings affecting security prices rapidly to reflect their new information. The combined effect of (a) information coming to the investor in a random and independent fashion and of (b) numerous participants in the market who adjust stock prices rapidly to reflect this new information is that price changes are independent and random. The net result in the market place is that security prices reflect all public information at any point and that the security prices prevailing at any point should be unbiased reflections of all currently available information. This thesis is closely related to the "random walk theory" which holds that any attempt to forecast future stock prices using past volume and price data is futile, and that future prices are random and independent of previous prices.[10]

One conclusion that can be reached after studying the assumptions and evidence regarding efficient markets is that the market is efficient for the majority of the investors. Even Ben Graham, known as the Father of Modern Securities Analysis, in his later years was a believer in "efficient markets." In an interview in 1976, Graham said:

> I am no longer an advocate of elaborate techniques of security analysis in order to find superior value opportunities. This was a rewarding activity, say, 40 years ago, when our textbook 'Graham and Dodd' was first published; but the situation has changed a good deal since then. In the old days any well-trained security analyst could do a good professional job of selecting undervalued issues through detailed studies; but in the light of the enormous amount of research now being carried on, I doubt whether in most cases such extensive efforts will generate sufficiently superior selections to justify their cost. To that very limited extent I'm on the side of the 'efficient market' school of thought now generally accepted by the professors.[11]

We would like to note here that two statistical tests have been done which indicate that the market is not efficient. If the market were truly efficient, it would not be possible to use any particular selection process and achieve superior results. These tests demonstrate, however, that by choosing low price to earnings ratio stocks an investor can achieve results better than the market without increasing his risk factor. In the next chapter, we begin to develop a philosophy that takes advantage of this inefficiency and that, if used properly, will allow investors to achieve well above average results on their investment portfolios.

Not only have the "random walk theory" and "efficient market hypothesis" led to the academic destruction of "technical analysis," they have led us on our search to "indexing" and "modern portfolio" theory.

"Indexing" is a logical conclusion and answer. After all, if the market is efficient and can't be beaten, why not join it? That's the whole idea of "indexing," i.e., structuring a portfolio after a market index, such as the Standard & Poor's 500 Index. In theory, as the market moves, so does the portfolio, since it is structured to represent the market.

Will its performance, however, be as good as the market's? Probably not. The portfolio has transaction costs the market does not have. And the portfolio responds to market changes and to industry weightings within a statistical index. It will not mirror exactly the market, but it *will be* responding to the market's changes.

This is an interesting way to manage money. The market can't be beaten. So an investment program is set up that will most certainly underperform the market—a prophecy fulfilled.

For those people who want to try to beat the market and are contemporary academicians, we have the "modern portfolio theory." How modern it is is open to debate. It began in 1952 when Harry M. Markowitz published his first article on portfolio analysis. For the first time, theory dealt with risk. Somehow an investor should value something as being worth less, the more risk it has.

The next contribution to the "modern portfolio theory" was by Tobin in 1958. Tobin observed that the ability to borrow and lend allows one to separate the portfolio selection process into the selection of a good combination of equities with leverage being used to tailor the mix to the client's attitude toward risk.

The next phase of evolution, beginning in the 1960s, dealt with markets being efficient and with the "equilibrium theory." This led to the idea that, in an efficient market, one should expect price behavior that is essentially random.

This latter approach suggests that the intrinsic value of a stock should follow a kind of random walk. It still, however, does not specify what value is. What the relationship is between present value and future prospects is the question addressed by the "capital asset pricing model." This is a model of the relationship between risk and return in a market that is efficient and in which knowledge is widely available and is incorporated into stock prices.[12]

The capital asset pricing model is used to determine the risk of a stock; this measurement is called the stock's Beta. The higher the Beta, the more risky the asset becomes. Beta refers to the volatility of an individual stock relative to a market index, usually the Standard & Poor's 500. The market has a Beta of 1. If a particular stock has a Beta of 1.5, the capital asset pricing model says the stock will be 50% more volatile than the market. In other words, if the market rises 10%, this particular stock should advance 15%. In summary, Modern Portfolio Theory focuses on the trade-off between risk and return, and measures risk based on price volatility rather than on the underlying value.

The top-down philosophy

If the "technical analysis theory" and the "modern portfolio theory" are philosophies that will not produce good results, then how about the "top-down approach"? This philosophy is based on a basic investment theory. A security's price reflects the earnings of the underlying corporation, related to the health of its industry, which is a result of macro-economic performance. The practitioner begins with a forecast of the national economy. From this forecast he determines those industries that should profit the most, given that ecnomic picture. Then, finally, those companies that will profit the most within those industries are selected for investment commitment.

The top-down method is the one the business schools would like to see succeed. It ties everything together very neatly. It encourages the basing of security selection on a logical series of decisions. Not only the business schools, but also the fund managers and their clients view this theory with favor.

It is interesting to observe how often meetings with clients involve a discussion of the economy, and of what the investment manager thinks will happen regarding interest rates, inflation, and the gross national product.

Although "top-down" can be a very marketable philosophy because of its logic and its sophisticated approach, it has had very little success as a workable investment philosophy. It is used frequently by large organizations, since it is believed that superior economic forecasting can identify industries and companies well in advance of their market moves. This approach can also facilitate the movement of large pools of money.

The bedrock of the "top-down" approach is not very strong. All one need do is recall the economic forecasts he has heard over the past several years. As poor as these forecasts have been, should one invest money on those premises? If the investor still has doubts, he should look at the record of well-known economic consulting firms. An article entitled "How the Forecasters Went Wrong in 1981" in the December 28, 1981, issue of *Business Week* reports:

> For the second consecutive year, the quarterly pattern of the gross national product looked nothing like the consensus forecast of a year earlier. The consensus forecast had called for little or no growth in the first quarter of 1981. Instead, fueled by a strong January, Gross National product jumped at a startling annual rate of 8.6%. As late as midyear, the consensus forecast compiled by Eggert Economic Enterprises called for growth of 3.4% in the fourth quarter. Estimates now project a dive of 5% for the quarter.[13]

Here, we raise the question: If the underlying economic forecast is not all that accurate, can this method be used to select prosperous industries and, finally, prosperous companies?

The bottom-up approach

A theory that disregards the economy and industry is called the "bottom-up" approach. Practitioners of this philosophy hope to identify companies whose stocks the analyst feels are cheap and will be recognized as such by the market in the not-too-distant future. When the market recognizes its valuation error, the portfolio manager is rewarded as the price rises to its correct value. A phrase often used by the analyst with this method is that "the stock is cheap." Generally, it is cheap based on (1) perceived asset value, or (2) perceived earning potential.

The bottom-up approach is generally used for smaller pools of money than the "top-down" approach or the "modern portfolio theory." Smaller pools of money allow the investment manager to choose stocks and form a portfolio from the bottom up. The portfolio manager usually will have some diversification by industry, and will pay very little attention to macro-economic forecasts. One issue the authors raise when talking to money managers who use this method is related to how they define "cheap."

We have found that "cheap stock" is a term most people have not formally defined. Often it refers to estimates of future earnings per share. People will discuss a stock in terms of what the company is doing and how much it will earn next year, or the year after that, in order that they may justify current prices based on earnings two years away. They will quote well-known Wall Street analysts and what others generally perceive for the stock in the distant future.

How accurate are earnings forecasts of well-intentioned analysts? How well do the Wall Street superstars do in their stock picking? These two questions are crucial to anyone who is practicing a "bottom-up" selection process. First, let's examine a test of forecasting earnings.

An interesting study by I.M.D. Little called "Higgledly Piggledly Growth" reported the earnings of British firms and found that changes followed a random walk. This meant that successive changes in earnings per share were statistically independent, and that the study of the sequence of historical changes in earnings per share was useless as an aid in predicting furture changes. In other words, historical rates of growth in earnings provide no clue to future rates of growth.

This work was attacked on methodological grounds, and Little and a colleague revised the work and expanded the coverage of their earlier work. Their conclusion was the same. Changes in earnings for British corporations followed a random walk.[14]

A similar study by Murphy, Linter, Glouber, and Brealey covering American companies (reported in the same source) found much the same result. American companies' earnings follow a random walk. In addition to showing that corporate earnings behave in a random manner, tests have also shown that earnings tend to follow a "naive extrapolation" of recent rates of change.

Despite this evidence, security analysts in many financial institutions produce forecasts of corporate earnings that do not differ significantly from those that would have been produced by the "naive extrapolation" of recent historical trends. In trying to form his own expectation regarding the future, the analyst finds this expectation being colored or constrained by reference to what has been happening recently.[14]

In yet another study, again from the same source, Cragg and Malkeel analyzed the accuracy of forecasts of earnings. Correlations betwen predicted and realized rates of growth were low, although most were significantly greater than zero. That study's main conclusion: Evidence accumulated recently shows that growth of earnings in past periods is not a useful predictor of future growth of earnings. The remarkable implication is that the careful estimates of the security analysts participating in this survey, the bases of which were not limited to public information, performed only a little better than those past rates of growth. Moreover, the market price-to-earnings ratios themselves were no better in forecasting future earnings growth than either the analyst's forecasts or the use of past rates of growth. In other words, a high P/E ratio (price-to-earnings ratio) does not necessarily signify high visible growth in earnings; nor do low P/E ratios indicate low or no growth. This is another statistical test we have used to formulate the low P/E ratio investing philosophy that will be developed further in the next chapter.

The conclusion of these studies predicting earnings is both encouraging and discouraging. The general failure of security analysts to predict earnings with any accuracy creates a great opportunity for anyone who *can* predict earnings accurately. The results also show that changes in earnings have a tendency to follow a random walk, and that historical earnings are useful in predicting levels of earnings. Absolute and exact changes, however, are extremely difficult to forecast.[14]

By now the reader should have an overview of professional money management and the major philosophies that are in practice. An organized summary of these philosophies should help the reader draw conclusions regarding their weaknesses.

The *Technical Analysis Theory* uses charts and other devices to aid the practitioner in forecasting future market and stock price moves.

The *Modern Portfolio Theory* measures and defines the risk of a particular stock in relation to the market. It compares risk-adjusted performances of various portfolios, and breaks a security's return into components showing that portion attributed to the market, beta, and that portion attributed to individual selection, alpha. This individual selection process identifies undervalued stocks in relation to their forecast value.

The *Top-Down Approach* begins with a forecast of the economy, then selects industries that should do well within that economic picture, and finally selects the best companies in those industries.

The *Bottom-Up Approach* focuses on stock selection and picks those that are expected to perform the best or that are undervalued the most. Usually, value is based on forecast or perceived earnings power or asset value.

We believe that each of these philosophies has two major weaknesses that cause them, on average, to give unacceptable returns.

First, they are all dependent on a forecast of some kind, whether it is the economy, estimates of earnings, or market moves. The fact is that no one can forecast the future.

Second, all these philosophies focus on the market or the stock and have a tendency to dismiss the underlying company as being the most important consideration. How often do we hear that Company XYZ's stock currently selling at $40 is going to be a $55 stock in the next six months? The reasons usually given are that its earnings are going to go from X to Z and that the market is undervaluing it. We believe that too much emphasis is placed on the movement of the stock's price and not enough on the underlying realities of the company. This is true no matter which philosophy is used.

In the next chapter we will present an investment philosophy that takes an approach opposite to those described above. First, this philosophy will rely very little on forecasting, and, second, it is based on currently measurable value. By implementing the philosophy we advocate, an investor will obtain a real rate of return on investment after allowing for inflation and taxes — a necessary step in accumulating wealth.

References

1. John Train, *Dance of the Money Bees: A Professional Speaks Frankly on Investing* (New York: Harper & Row, 1974), p. 3.
2. David Dreman, *Contrarian Investment Strategy: The Psychology of Stock Market Success* (New York: Random House, 1979), pp. 57-59.
3. Charles Ellis, "The Losers Game," *Financial Analysts Journal,* July-August 1975, p. 19.
4. "Firms Turn to Basics in Slack Bond Market," *Pension & Investment Age,* February 20, 1984, p. 17.
5. John Train, *The Money Masters* (New York: Harper & Row, 1980), p. 219.
6. Eugene F. Fama, "The Behavior of Stock Market Prices," *Journal of Business,* January 1965, pp. 34-105.
7. William F. Sharpe, "Likely Gains From Market Timing," *Financial Analysts Journal,* March-April 1975, p. 67.
8. Dreman, p. 29.
9. Benjamin Graham, *The Intelligent Investor: A Book of Practical Counsel,* 4th ed. rev. (New York: Harper & Row, 1973), p. x.
10. Frank K. Reilly, *Investment Analysis and Portfolio Management* (Hinsdale, Ill.: Dryden Press, 1979), pp. 162-186.
11. Charles D. Ellis, "Ben Graham: Ideas as Mementos," *Financial Analysts Journal,* July-August 1982, p. 47.
12. William F. Sharpe, "Evolution of Modern Portfolio Theory," *C.F.A. Readings in Financial Analysis,* 5th ed., The Institute of Chartered Financial Analysts (Homewood, Ill.: Richard D. Irwin 1981), pp. 256-260.
13. "How the Forecasters Went Wrong in 1981," *Business Week,* December 28, 1981, p. 85.
14. James H. Lorie and Mary T. Hamilton, *The Stock Market: Theories and Evidence* (Homewood, Ill.: Richard D. Irwin, 1973).

CHAPTER 2

The Low P/E-Ratio Approach to Investing

After examining the various philosophies in use by professional money managers, we found only one successful approach, one that consistently provided above-average results. This approach centers on buying a diversified group of stocks with below-average price-to-earnings, P/E, ratios. What follows is a discussion on what price-to-earnings ratios are and how they fit into an investment program.

A price-to-earnings ratio is a number calculated by dividing the price per share of a company's stock by its earnings per share for the most recent 12 months. This calculation provides the investor with a ratio of price-to-earnings for a company which can now be compared to other company price-to-earnings ratios. Once these ratios are calculated for a large universe of common stocks, for example, the New York Stock Exchange listed companies, the investor can divide these stocks into deciles ranked from lowest to highest by their price-to-earnings ratios.

The low P/E-ratio approach to investing is to choose a representative group of companies from the bottom three deciles, or the lowest 30% of all P/E ratios. Problems arise with cyclical companies having very low P/E ratios because their earnings are at a cyclical peak, or very high P/E ratios because their earnings are at a cyclical trough. Such problems are resolved by normalizing the company's earnings per share.[1] This can be done by calculating an average return on total capital over a period of several years and deriving a per-share earnings figure from the average. Companies with no loss years can be relied upon more than companies that do have loss years, even though they both may have the same average return on total assets calculated for a several-year period.

Another aspect of the price-to-earnings ratio is its reciprocal, which is known as the "earnings yield." The earnings yield is calculated simply by dividing the price-to-earnings ratio into 1. For example, a company with a $10 stock price and $2 of earnings per share has a price-to-earnings ratio of 5. This ratio of 5 is converted to an earnings yield by dividing 1 by 5 for a 20% earnings yield. The common stock's earnings yield is comparable to the yield on fixed-income investments, giving the investor a benchmark of relative value. The idea is to buy stocks of a group of companies with the lowest price-to-earnings ratios or the highest earnings yields.

Our observation is that the most successful investors are *value investors,* who concentrate on cheap stocks out of favor with Wall Street. Value investing focuses on buying an asset for less than its intrinsic value. Intrinsic value is best defined in Ben Graham's *Security Analysis* textbook as:

> That value which is justified by the facts, e.g., assets, earnings, dividends, definite prospects, including the factor of management. The primary objective in using the adjective "intrinsic" is to empha-size the distinction between value and current market price, but not to invest this "value" with an aura of permanence. In truth, the com-puted intrinsic value is likely to change at least from year to year, as the various factors governing that value are modified. But in most cases intrinsic value changes less rapidly and drastically than market price, and the investor usually has an opportunity to profit from any wide discrepancy between the current price and the intrinsic value as determined at the same time (p. 27).

Value investors point to several definable value benchmarks. Some of these are price-to-earnings, price-to-sales, price-to-depreciation, or price-to-book value. Other investors use hidden assets not appearing in a corporation's annual report at current values, or Ben Graham's favorite, net-working capital, in which one buys the company stock for its minimum liquidating value.

S. Francis Nicholson, a practitioner and researcher of value techniques, men-tions several of these value benchmarks in his article, "Price-Ratios in Relation to Investment Results."[2] Those mentioned were price-to-earnings, price-to-depreciation, price-to-sales, and price-to-book-value. All the value benchmarks had good performance records over time. The most statistically significant price-to-earnings ratios, are shown below with historical performance figures. (More will be said about Nicholson's study in Chapter 4.)

Table 2-1. Annual earnings related to mean prices.

Grouped According to Quintiles in Each Year 1937 to 1962 Inclusive	Average Price Appreciation Percentages						
	After 1 yr. %	2 yr. %	3 yr. %	4 yr. %	5 yr. %	6 yr. %	7 yr. %
A Lowest price-earnings ratios	16	34	55	76	98	125	149
B Next higher	9	22	34	48	65	82	100
C Next higher	7	18	30	43	60	77	96
D Next higher	6	14	24	35	50	65	83
E Highest price-earnings ratios	3	11	21	31	46	65	84

Comment: With the large number of items and periods averaged above, the pattern of price changes seems remarkably consistent. The performance of the A group after four years was best in 22 out of 23 years. The worst performance after four years occurred in the E group in 13 years, and in the D group in 6 years.

Source: Nicholson, "Price Ratios in Relation to Investment Results."

Why did we choose price-to-earnings ratios as our main value benchmark? In our opinion, price-to-earnings ratios are easily obtainable and easy to apply. Moreover, there is over 60 years of empirical evidence proving that, in fact, low price-to-earnings ratio stocks outperform high price-to-earnings ratio stocks and the general market averages. Some of this evidence will be cited in this chapter, more in chapter 4. For those who want exhaustive proof of the efficacy of the low price-to-earnings ratio philosophy, several additional studies are presented in Appendix C.

Benjamin Graham—an early practitioner

Benjamin Graham, known as the founder of the low price-to-earnings ratio, or value approach to investing, was both practitioner and researcher in the investment field.

In the revised 1973 edition of the *Intelligent Investor,* Graham cites a study done at Drexel & Company by Paul Miller on the price performance of the 30 Dow Jones stocks grouped by price-to- earnings ratios.[3] This study covered a 32-year time span, 1937 through 1969.

Table 2-2. Average annual percentage gain or loss on test issues, 1937-69.

Period	10 Low-Multiplier Issues	10 High-Multiplier Issues	30 DJIA Stocks
1937-1942	− 2.2	− 10.0	− 6.3
1943-1947	17.3	8.3	14.9
1948-1952	16.4	4.6	9.9
1953-1957	20.9	10.0	13.7
1958-1962	10.2	− 3.3	3.6
1963-1969 (8 years)	8.0	4.6	4.0

Source: Graham, *The Intelligent Investor,* 4th ed.

Each year the 30 Dow Jones Stocks were divided into two groups, the 10 lowest price-to-earnings ratio stocks, and the 10 highest. These two groups were also compared to the Dow Jones average of 30 stocks.

The cumulative price performance is shown in Table 2-2 for the years 1937 through 1969. The test period covered 34 one-year holding periods.

The low P/E-ratio stocks outperformed the Dow Jones Industrial averages in 25 of the 34 years. In six of the years, the low P/E-ratio stocks did about the same as the averages, and, in three of the years, underperformed the averages. Table 2-2 presents the data in five-year periods, which shows the consistently better performance of the low P/E-ratio stocks than either the high P/E-ratio stocks or the 30 Dow stocks average.

Table 2-3 takes the performance results from Paul Miller's study for each of the three groups: low P/E-ratio stocks, high P/E-ratio stocks, and the 30 Dow Jones stocks. The study assumes an investment of $10,000 in each group beginning in 1936.

Table 2-3. Performance of low P/E-ratio group compared: 1936 through 1962.

Original Investment	Low P/E Stocks	High P/E Stocks	30 Dow Jones Stocks
$10,000	$66,000	$25,300	$44,000

Source: Graham, *The Intelligent Investor,* 4th ed.

The table shows the superior results of low P/E-ratio stock selection over time.

David Dreman—a modern-day practitioner

A more recent practitioner and advocate of the low price-to-earnings-ratio philosophy is David Dreman. In his 1979 edition of *Contrarian Investment Strategy,* Dreman cites several statistical studies which show low price-to-earnings-ratio stocks outperforming higher price-to-earnings-ratio stocks, as well as the performance of the group as a whole.[4] One of the most important studies included a sample of 1,251 companies, 70% of which were listed on the New York Stock Exchange. The time period of the study was August 1968 to August 1977.

Switching stocks quarterly showed the best results. But, even if the portfolio were held for the full nine-year period, the results were much above average for the low P/E-ratio groups and below average for the high P/E-ratio groups.

Table 2-4. Annualized compound rates of return: August 1968-August 1977 (full period of study).

Stocks Ranked by P/E Multiples Decile*	Switching Stocks After Each:				Holding Original Portfolio for 9 Years
	1 Quarter	6 Months	1 Year	3 Years	
1 (highest)	− 2.64%	− 1.06%	− 1.13%	− 1.43%	0.33%
2...............	0.92	1.62	0.56	− 0.28	1.27
3...............	0.51	0.62	1.63	0.85	3.30
4...............	3.06	3.42	3.31	4.87	5.36
5...............	2.19	4.46	2.93	5.02	3.72
6...............	4.84	5.33	6.70	4.82	4.52
7...............	7.90	6.07	6.85	5.89	6.08
8...............	8.83	8.24	8.56	7.78	6.35
9...............	11.85	8.40	6.08	7.73	6.40
10 (lowest)	14.00	11.68	10.26	10.89	7.89

Average return of sample....................4.75%

* Take all stocks in study and divide them into ten groups according to the price-to-earnings multiple.

Source: Dreman, *Contrarian Investment Strategy.*

The results become even more vivid when they are converted into dollars and are compounded at the rates of return shown in Table 2-4.

In Dreman's study, the compounding effect had a dramatic impact on portfolio performance over time, as shown in Table 2-5. The low P/E-ratio group at best tripled, and at worst doubled, while the high P/E-ratio group at best was flat and at worst was down 23%.

Table 2-5. Results: Low and high P/E-ratio groups.

	Performance: Switching Quarterly	
	August 1968	August 1977
Lowest P/E-ratio-decile	$10,000	$32,519
Highest P/E-ratio-decile	$10,000	$ 7,708

	Performance: Switching Yearly	
	August 1968	August 1977
Lowest P/E-ratio-decile	$10,000	$24,086
Highest P/E-ratio-decile	$10,000	$ 9,038

	Performance: Holding for Full 9 Years	
	August 1968	August 1977
Lowest P/E-ratio-decile	$10,000	$19,824
Highest P/E-ratio-decile	$10,000	$10,306

Source: Bowen and Ganucheau.

In the search for an investment strategy that is workable and that produces results, the discovery of low P/E-ratio stock selection was extremely important. When all other strategies were failing, it was refreshing to find one that was easy to apply and that had stood the test of time.

After researching the work of Ben Graham, David Dreman, and many others, we decided to try the low P/E-ratio philosophy. We constructed a model portfolio on January 1, 1982.

We obtained a list of stocks in the Standard & Poor's 500 for December 31, 1981, ranked by their price-to-earnings ratios. A Standard & Poor's Stock Guide was used next to differentiate the stocks by quality. The Stock Guide has a column listing quality ratings based on earnings, dividend stability, and dividend growth. We selected only those companies with a rating of A – or higher.

The next criterion we used to reduce the size of the list was yield. Each stock must have had a yield equal to 40% of the prevailing bond yield. The idea in constructing this list was to put together a portfolio of stocks that were cheap, that were of high quality and that would provide above-average income.

To give diversification, the portfolio had 22 companies from 14 industries.

The portfolio was then put aside for one year. No economic forecasts were involved. No market timing was used, since we were 100% invested in equal amounts among the stocks.

The results over the next 12 months were interesting and informative. The total return—price appreciation plus dividends—for the portfolio over the year was +25% versus +20.3% for the Standard & Poor's 500. Given the fact that 1982 was the worst recession year since World War II, who would have thought that Boeing would be up 50.6%; Borden, Inc., up 70.1%; J. C. Penney up 69%; and West Point Pepperell up 67.8%.

These are a few of the surprising results in the portfolio. (The entire list, showing the returns for each stock, is given in chapter 10.) We realize that these are results for only one year. However, as indicated, numerous studies indicate that future results can be expected to be similar to those experienced by these stocks.

Conclusion

We believe the price-to-earnings ratio is the most useful benchmark of value. Clearly it's most readily available and easy to apply. The research on its reliability and consistency of results has been exhaustive, covering a period of 68 years and 16 different practitioners. Three of the most prominent researchers were cited in this chapter. As we proceed, more research will be presented to show the types of results the investor can expect to obtain.

First, however, we will answer the question we believe was previously unanswered as to the financial reason this approach produces superior investment results.

References

1. Benjamin Graham, David L. Dodd, and Sidney Cottle, *Security Analysis: Principles and Technique,* 4th ed. (New York: McGraw-Hill, 1962), pp. 468-477.
2. Francis Nicholson, "Price Ratios in Relation to Investment Results," *Financial Analysts Journal,* January-February 1968, p. 105.
3. Benjamin Graham, *The Intelligent Investor: A Book of Practical Counsel,* 4th ed. (New York: Harper & Row, 1973), p. 80.
4. David Dreman, *Contrarian Investment Strategy: The Psychology of Stock Market Success* (New York: Random House, 1979), p. 131.

CHAPTER 3

Why Does This Approach Work?

The discovery about low P/E-ratio stocks has become a key piece in the puzzle of formulating an investment philosophy. Why do low P/E-ratio stock selection methods work? Even in the studies testing the "efficient market" hypothesis, the price-to-earnings ratio was one of the few indicators that could provide above-average results and could disprove the "efficient market" hypothesis.

David Dreman in his book, *Contrarian Investment Strategy,* discusses some of the major factors that determine a stock's price. He mentions one study whose results indicate that stock prices depend strongly on changes in absolute earnings and changes in earnings in relation to analysts' estimates. It is evident that correct estimates of earnings are of enormous value in the selection of stocks.[1]

Dreman discusses more studies that show the differences between managements' and analysts' estimates of earnings and how each estimate differs from actual results. Although his studies show managements' estimates are closer to the actual results than analysts' estimates, neither is generally accurate enough to be relied upon (Dreman, p. 144). Managements' estimates have a mean error of 14½%, while analysts' estimates have a mean error of 16.6%.

The market has a tendency to pay more, that is, a higher price-to-earnings multiple, for those companies that appear to have more growth in earnings. As Dreman's studies show, it is impossible to forecast earnings with any degree of consistency. Dreman concludes,

. . . If one can not forecast with any degree of accuracy then the range between high and low P/E multiples should be much narrower. But the range usually is not and because it is not, the road to investment opportunity is wide open. Stocks trading at low P/E multiples will have the same probabilities of large positive earnings gains as stocks trading at high P/E multiples. Consequently you have to question the market's ability to forecast future earnings (Dreman, p. 149).

Assume for a moment that earnings can be forecast with some degree of confidence. The other criterion needed to determine a future price for a particular stock is the price-to-earnings multiple. A study by Frank K. Reilly and Eugene F. Dryumski, determined that there is more volatility in the earnings' multiple over time than in the earnings' trends.[2] The multiple the market is willing to pay for a company's earnings is more volatile than its earnings' trend, which most researchers have shown moves in a "random walk."

If analysts could forecast earnings, the question of whether it matters could be raised, since the multiple the market will pay for those earnings can be so volatile. Analysts identify, and the market participants bid up the P/E ratios, i.e., of those companies that appear to have high, above-average, sustainable growth. High P/E ratios are often justified on the basis of "high visability of growth in earnings."

In a book titled *Competitive Strategy,* Michael E. Porter argues that,

> Competition in an industry continually works to drive down the rates of return on invested capital toward the competitive floor rate of return, or the return that would be earned by the economists' perfectly competitive industry. This competitive floor or free market return is approximated by the yield on long term government securities adjusted upward by the risk of capital loss.[3]

What is caused by investors in the stock market is the driving to extremes of securities' prices based on perceived or forecast results, rather than on the underlying realities of the businesses. This drives multiples upward for some and downward for others, and the gap between the extremes is too large. As companies' results trend toward the mean in reality, their securities' prices react accordingly. Those prices that were too optimistic decline as reality sets in, and those that were too pessimistic rise. This regression to the mean or average explains the psychological reason low P/E-ratio stocks as a group outperform high P/E-ratio stocks as a group.

Another way to understand how low P/E-ratio strategies produce above-average results is to consider them from a financial-return perspective. For this, several terms and concepts need to be presented.

(1) *Equity per share,* or *book value per share* consists of the sum of common stock plus capital surplus plus retained earnings divided by the number of shares outstanding. The value of common stock, as it appears on the books of a company, is simply a par or stated value arbitrarily assigned to the common shares. This figure may or may not represent, or even closely resemble, what the original stockholders paid for their interests in the company. *Paid in capital* in excess of par is the amount paid in by the common stockholders in excess of the par value of their shares. *Retained earnings* consist of the profits of past years that have been invested in the company instead of being paid out in dividends to stockholders. *Book value* refers to that amount that has been contributed to the corporation by the shareholders either through stock subscription or through reinvestment since the formation of the corporation.

(2) *Return on equity* is the ratio or percentage that shows how much the company is earning on funds contributed by stockholders after all expenses including interest.[4]

(3) *Net profit* or *earnings* represents what a company has left after meeting all costs of a year's operation. It is the amount technically available to pay dividends on the perferred and common stock and to use in the operation of the business. Net earnings not paid out in dividends are shown as *retained earnings.* (Christy, Roden, p. 215.)

These three terms have a very close relationship. If two of the values are known, the third can be calculated. Book value multiplied by return on equity equals earnings; earnings divided by book value equals return on equity, and so forth. The three terms become very important to the investor.

Assume that a corporation is formed. One person contributes $100,000 to it and is the sole owner. Assume also that the corporation has no debt or preferred stock outstanding. Its capital structure is all equity. Next, assume that the corporation earns, after taxes, $15,000 on its equity. Let's say the assets consumed during the period of production through depreciation and other means have been replaced, so that the business can continue.

The corporation has generated a 15% return on the stockholders' beginning equity, that is,

$$\frac{\$\ 15,000}{\$100,000} = 15\%$$

If the corporation pays none of these earnings in dividends, it will begin its next fiscal year with stockholders' equity of $115,000.

In this example, at the end of year one, the owner leaves his earnings in the corporation, and these retained earnings, along with the other assets, continue to earn 15%. The corporation's earnings for the next year will be $17,250, that is, 15% of $115,000. If the corporation can be expected to continue to generate returns of 15%, and the owner sells his equity at book value— $115,000—he will be selling his interest at 6.66 times earnings:

$$\frac{\$115,000}{\$\ 17,250} = 6.66.$$

The buyer will recieve $115,000 worth of productive assets that can earn a 15% return, for which he pays 6.66 times earnings. Thus, book value, return on equity, and P/E ratio are all related. It becomes evident that the investor buys the *earnings stream* of the corporation.

The main conclusion of our first chapter was that most people in the investment business attempt to forecast stock prices and make money by buying and selling based on those forecasts of moves in stock prices. Also, people mentally segregate the stock from the underlying business, allowing themselves to be influenced by dramatic changes in price and forget the underlying realities of the business in which they are part owner. Ben Graham had an interesting overall view of common stocks:

> Common stocks have one important investment characteristic and one important speculative characteristic. Their investment value and average market price tend to increase irregularly but persistently over the decades as their net worth builds up through the reinvestment of undistributed earnings—incidentally, with no clear cut plus or minus response to inflation. However, most of the time common stocks are subject to irrational and excessive price fluctuations in both directions as the consequence of the ingrained tendency of most people to speculate or gamble—i.e., to give way to hope, fear and greed.[5]

In the previous example, we assumed that the earnings of the corporation were retained by the corporation and invested in productive assets that would generate a 15% return. Combining this with what Graham observed, one can see the beginning of the accumulation of wealth through the retention of earnings and through compound interest.

One of the most potent powers in the world is not associated with any government. It is the power of compound interest. Money allowed to compound can grow to staggering sums in the span of one generation or even in a decade, if the rate is sufficiently high. For example, $1,000 compounding year after year at 15% will amount to $23,455,491 in 72 years, the life expectancy of the average man.

Is 15% sustainable? Perhaps, but let us assume a return of 9%, the figure most studies use for the long-term rate of return for common stocks.[6] At this rate, $1,000 compounds to $495,117 in 72 years, a half million dollars. Not only is the effect of compounding impressive, but these examples point out the dramatic effect of the rate at which interest is compounding. For a full discussion on compound interest and bond investment, you ought to look at *Inside the Yield Book* by Sidney Homer and Martin Leibowitz: "Compounding occurs not only in fixed income investments, but also in the compounding of retained earnings by business enterprises."[7] (More about bonds, stocks, and compounding later.)

In the example given earlier, we assumed that the owner of the corporation would sell his interest at book value, and that the price was 6.66 times earnings to generate a 15% return on investment for the purchaser. As Graham observes, however, market prices fluctuate dramatically based on fear or greed. How do these differences in price, above or below book value, affect the rate of return realized by the investor?

For the first example, assume a stock sells at book value, retains all its earnings and has a sustainable return on equity of 15%. Book value and earnings would grow as follows.

Table 3-1. Company 1. Internal reinvestment rate = return on equity times earnings retention rate, 15% × 100% = 15%.

Book value $30
Price $30
Dividend yield 0

	Year				
	1	2	3	4	5
Beginning book value	30.00	34.50	39.68	45.62	52.47
Earnings (book value times return on equity	4.50	5.18	5.95	6.84	7.87
End-of-year book value	34.50	39.68	45.62	52.47	60.34

Note: The asset value, i.e., book value, compounds at the rate of return on equity, 15%. Thus, $30.00 compounding at 15% per year becomes $60.34 in five years.

Now, assume that the stock sells at book value with a return on equity of 15%, pays out 40% of its earnings in dividends, and that retained earnings and dividends are both reinvested at 15%.

Table 3-2. Company 2. Internal reinvestment rate = return on equity times earnings retention rate,
15% × .60 = 9%; yield: 6%; total return: 15%.

Book value $30
Price $30
Dividend yield $1.80/30 = 6%

	Year				
	1	2	3	4	5
Beginning book value	30.00	32.70	35.64	38.85	42.35
Earnings per share (book value times return on equity)	4.50	4.90	5.35	5.83	6.35
Retained earnings (.60 times earnings per share)	2.70	2.94	3.21	3.50	3.81
Dividend (.40 times earnings per share)	1.80	1.96	2.14	2.33	2.54
Book value at end of year	32.70	35.64	38.85	42.35	46.16

The dividends can be reinvested at 15% to compound as follows:

	Yr. 2		Yr. 3		Yr. 4		Yr. 5		
First year's dividend . . . . 1.80 +	15%	+	15%	+	15%	+	15%	=	3.15
Second year's dividend . . .	1.96	+	15%	+	15%	+	15%	=	2.98
Third year's dividend			2.14	+	15%	+	15%	=	2.83
Fourth year's dividend					2.33	+	15%	=	2.68
Fifth year's dividend							2.54		2.54

Total dividend received plus interest
earned on dividend 14.18
Fifth year's book value . . . .   +46.16
Total return 60.34

Note: At what rate would $30 compound to 60.34 in five years? The rate would be 15%.

In this example, the investor would be indifferent about whether the company paid a dividend or retained the earnings. Earnings retained can be reinvested internally at 15% (the return on equity), while earnings distributed as dividends can be reinvested in bonds yielding 15%. These reinvestment assumptions hold true for all the examples, and we assume the investment is not subject to taxes.

Next, assume that a stock sells at 75% of book value with a return on equity of 15% and a 40% dividend payout that can be reinvested at 15%.

Table 3-3. Company 3. Internal reinvestment rate 9%; yield: 8%; total return: 17%.

Book value $30.00
Market Value $22.50
Dividend yield $1.80/$22.50   =   8%

	Year				
	1	2	3	4	5
Beginning book value	30.00	32.70	35.64	38.85	42.35
Earnings	4.50	4.90	5.35	5.83	6.35
Retained earnings	2.70	2.94	3.21	3.50	3.81
Dividend	1.80	1.96	2.14	2.33	2.54
End-of-year book value	32.70	35.64	38.85	42.35	46.16

The dividends can be reinvested at 15% to compound as follows:

	Yr. 2		Yr. 3		Yr. 4		Yr. 5		
First year's dividend . . . . .1.80 +	15%	+	15%	+	15%	+	15%	=	3.15
Second year's dividend . . .	1.96	+	15%	+	15%	+	15%	=	2.98
Third year's dividend			2.14	+	15%	+	15%	=	2.83
Fourth year's dividend					2.33	+	15%	=	2.68
Fifth year's dividend							2.54		2.54

Total dividend received plus interest earned on dividend	14.18
Fifth year's book value times 75%, 46.16 times .75	+34.62
Total value received	$ 48.80

Note: At what rate would $22.50 compound to $48.80 in five years? The rate would be 16.74%.

This last example shows a stock that sells at 125% of book value, with a return on equity of 15% and a 40% dividend payout that can be reinvested at 15% (Table 3-4).

These examples of the compounding of asset values and returns show several important items. In the first two examples, both investments had a 15% return per year over the five-year period. In the third example, however, when the stock sold at 75% of book value, the investor received a higher return the first year, 17%, because of the higher yield.

Table 3-4. Company 4. Internal reinvestment rate: 9%; yield: 4.8%; total return: 13.8%.

Book value $30.00
Price $37.50
Dividend yield . . $1.80/$37.50 = 4.8%

	Year				
	1	2	3	4	5
Beginning book value	30.00	32.70	35.64	38.85	42.35
Earnings	4.50	4.90	5.35	5.83	6.35
Retained earnings	2.70	2.94	3.21	3.50	3.81
Dividend	1.80	1.96	2.14	2.33	2.54
End-of-year book value	32.70	35.64	38.85	42.35	46.16

The dividends can be reinvested at 15% to compound as follows:

	Yr. 2		Yr. 3		Yr. 4		Yr. 5		
First year's dividend . . . . .1.80 +	15%	+	15%	+	15%	+	15%	=	3.15
Second year's dividend . . .	1.96	+	15%	+	15%	+	15%	=	2.98
Third year's dividend			2.14	+	15%	+	15%	=	2.83
Fourth year's dividend					2.33	+	15%	=	2.68
Fifth year's dividend							2.54		2.54

Total dividend received plus interest
earned on dividend 14.18
Fifth year's book value times 1.25%,
46.16 times 1.25 . . . .   + 57.70
Total value . . . . $ 71.88

Note: At what rate would $37.50 compound to $71.88 in five years? The rate would be 13.9%.

The five-year compound rate of return was 16.7%, even though the stock continued to sell at 75% of its book value. This higher return was attributable to the higher initial return of 17%, but was diluted over the five-year period, since all money was reinvested at 15%.

In the fourth example, the initial return was the lowest at 13.8%, because it had a lower dividend yield when purchased. Through reinvestment, the five-year compound return rises to 13.9%.

The conclusion that can be drawn from these examples is that, where the reinvestment rates are the same for different companies, one receives more for his invested dollar when he purchases a stock below book value. Notice also that since equity per share multiplied by return on equity equals earnings, a purchase below book value results in the acquisition of a low P/E-ratio stock when the return on equity is a competitive rate.

Taking these observations to their logical conclusions, let's assume that all four companies can produce a sustainable return on equity of 15%, and that all other factors are equal. The market has mispriced companies 3 and 4. If company 3 regresses to book value at the end of the five-year period, it will have a five-year compound rate of return of 21.8%, consisting of 9% internal growth plus a dividend plus the narrowing of the discount to book value.

On the other hand, if the high P/E-ratio stock, company 4, regresses to book value, its five-year compound rate of return will be 9.98%, consisting of 9% internal growth plus a dividend plus the narrowing of the premium to book value. The difference between price and book value will be reduced by 25%, lowering the total realized return.

As mentioned before, the market, through expectations, drives security prices to extreme inefficiencies, creating the opportunities described. This is another reason low P/E-ratio stocks, on a group basis, can provide above-average results. As one author states this crucially important point:

> For purposes of computing the return on investment a distinction must be drawn between the investment base of an enterprise and that of an investor. The investor's investment base is the price he paid for his equity securities. Except for those cases in which he acquired such securities at book value, his investment base is going to differ from that of the company in which he has invested.[8]

The investor's return will be more or less than the return earned by the company, depending on whether he paid above or below book value for his stock.

The meaning of book value in investing is often overlooked or not clearly understood. Book value has been defined as the amount of capital that has been contributed by the shareholders, either through equity subscriptions or earnings reinvestment. Often, people will argue that it is a meaningless figure, that it in no way represents the real asset value of the company.

When discussing a company with low profitability in a mature industry, critics of book value will remark that the company could not be liquidated for anything close to book value. Conversely, when talking about a very profitable company, critics will argue the company could not be duplicated for that amount.

What these critics fail to consider is that book value is an accounting concept, or measure, as is net income. Therefore, book value and earnings determine return on equity, which is the measure of return that the stockholder is entitled to receive on his share of invested capital.

In our examples, we always assumed a fairly high sustainable return on equity and showed the worth building up through compounding. The investor needs to be aware of book value and the amount earned on it, because these measures help him to compare alternative investments to the equity being considered.

In an article entitled, "The Place of Book Value in Common Stock Evaluation," Frank E. Block comments that the rate of return earned on the common stock equity and the portion of those earnings that is retained are fundamental to the analysis of common stocks. This is because the retention of a part of earnings is the most common way in which book value is increased. The rate at which book value per share grows tends to set a long-term limit on the rate at which earnings per share can grow.[9]

Also, when the return on equity is greater than the return demanded by the market—bond yields or earnings yields of equities—the investor profits by having earnings retained and reinvested by the corporation at a rate higher than can be obtained by the individual if he receives a dividend and reinvests it himself.

Conversely, Block says, when the return on equity is below that of alternative investments, the individual profits by having all the earnings paid to him and reinvesting in the higher external opportunities.

Book value and the return it generates—return on equity—play a significant role in contemporary investment decisions, even though book value may not realistically represent the value of the corporate assets. The concept provides a method to compare the compounding rate for alternative investments.

An article, "The Concept of Sustainable Growth," by Guilford C. Babcock, concludes that earnings retained and added to book value are the key to growth.[10] Babcock argues that the earnings per share of any company for any period of time may be expressed as the product of five factors:

1. The profit margin on sales.
2. The turnover of sales to capital.
3. The effect of any debt employed—once the cost of debt is covered, the return it generates flows to the equity holder.
4. The tax rate.
5. Equity or book value per share.

Any change in earnings can be attributed to any one or a combination of these factors. There are limits, however, to all the factors except book value and the retention of earnings to build up book value. Companies' profit margins are determined by competition with other companies and with competing products. The government regulates taxes. There is only so much debt a company can incur, and assets can only be worked so hard.

The point is, for growth to occur, these four factors need to be maintained or improved. Once they have reached their most efficient or optimum levels, the only source left is to increase the equity base. The cheapest and most efficient way to do this is through the retention of earnings. Earnings-retention-to-book-value is very important for sustained growth (Babcock, p. 144) and for increases in shareholder wealth.

Investor Warren Buffett makes an interesting comparison of stocks and bonds. In his article, "How Inflation Swindles The Equity Investor," he contends that, in economic substance, stocks are very similar to bonds.

This belief may seem eccentric at first to most investors, since the return on a bond is fixed by the coupon rate, while the return on equity can vary substantially from one year to the next. However, if one examines the aggregate returns that have been earned by companies during the postwar years, he will discover that the returns on equity have, in fact, not varied much at all. As inflation has increased, the return on equity capital has not. Those who buy equities receive securities with an underlying fixed return, as do those who buy bonds.[11]

Despite the fixed-return similarity, several characteristics still differentiate stocks from bonds. The bondholder receives his coupon income in cash. He is left to reinvest the proceeds as best he can. Bonds mature and the coupon can be renegotiated, whereas stocks are perpetual and never mature. With stocks, part of the earnings is paid out in dividends and part is retained and reinvested at whatever rate the company is earning.

According to a more recent article, Buffett still believes that equities and bonds are fixed-return investments and that both suffer in periods of rising prices (Greenebaum, "Gauging the Market's Prospects," *Fortune Magazine,* Time, Inc., January 1983). He adds that the Dow Jones Industrial Average should be thought of as a 13% coupon bond. [12] Obviously, then, the price the investor pays for his holdings in relation to book value will affect significantly his long-term rate of return. Stocks purchased at or below book value will return more over long time periods than those purchased above book value.

The view that stocks and bonds are similar is somewhat different from conventional wisdom. Most people believe that bonds are for income, stocks are for growth. They argue that stocks, unlike bonds, are a good hedge against inflation, because the return on equity increases in an inflationary environment as profits rise, protecting the equity investor.

As Buffett pointed out, this does not appear to be the case. Other studies, such as those reported in "Inflation, Return on Equity and Stock Prices,"[13] present evidence that the Fortune 500 companies did not increase their return on equity enough during more recent time periods to offset the higher rates of inflation. As a result, their stockholders suffered accordingly (Fuller and

Petry, pp. 19-20). Those studies attribute the shortfall to the inability of companies to hold profit margins during inflationary periods (Fuller and Petry, p. 24). (In chapter 5, we discuss in more detail the effects inflation has on investing, and the effect inflation has on corporate earning power in chapter 8.)

Now that several comparisons have been drawn between stocks and bonds, the reader can understand why bonds can sometimes be more attractive than equities, and vice versa. If bonds are not, in the traditional view, considered as being for income only—whereby the coupon income is consumed—but rather as vehicles for growth in which the coupon income is reinvested, some interesting comparisons can be made.

A 12% coupon bond whose income can be reinvested in 12% bonds will double the investor's wealth in 6.11 years. The key to bond investment is the reinvestment rate. Some investors mistakenly expect that a bond purchased at a given yield will always produce that rate as a realized compound yield over the entire life of the bond. If future reinvestment rates during the life of the bond are less than the yield at the time of purchase, then the realized compound yield for the entire life of the bond will be less than the yield at the time of purchase. If future rates are higher than the yield at the time of purchase, then the realized compound yield will be more than the yield at the time of purchase.[14]

The risk in buying high-coupon bonds during periods of high interest rates is that rates could fall with the result that the reinvestment rate would decrease the investor's compounding effect. The equity investor, however, does not have this problem, because the return on equity is a generally static 12 to 13% for most companies. The reinvestment rate is locked in for the retained earnings portion of the earnings income.

An example applying the principles discussed here will demonstrate the value for the investor from low P/E-ratio stocks. Currently, high technology and communication stocks are in vogue, while consumer staple stocks are not. An investor can acquire shares in R.J. Reynolds Industries at $45½, 5.5 times the earnings estimated for 1983 and 6.5 times the actual earnings for 1982. Book value on December 31, 1982, is $43.10; the stock sells at 1.05 times book value. During the past five years, the return on equity has averaged 17% and is projected to average 17% over the next several years. (Estimates and statistics are from the Value Line Investment Survey.[15])

An investor in R.J. Reynolds Industries stock receives, for every dollar invested, earnings (an annuity) of 18¢, which will compound at 16.7% per year. This growth rate is arrived at by dividing the net income into two parts: reinvested earnings and dividends. The retained earnings can continue to grow at 17%,

---

Table 3-5. Weighted average total return.

The earnings annuity, P/E ratio of 5.5 = 1/5.5, is $.18 for every dollar.

Estimated earnings per share for 1983 = $8.30 $3.10 will be paid in dividends (37%)

$5.10 will be retained   (63%)

The retained earnings can compound at 17% . . . . .63 × 17 = 10.7%

Dividends can purchase stock at 1.05 times book
value and sustainable return on equity is 17% $\frac{17}{1.05}$ = 16.6 × .37 =   6.0%

Weighted average total return 16.7%

---

and, it is assumed, dividends can purchase more stock at 1.05 times book value. A weighted average of the two figures is calcuated to arrive at 16.7%.

The 18¢ annuity compounding at 16.7% will grow to $1.00 in 4.25 years. If the stock still sells at 1.05 times book value, the original investment including dividends will have doubled in just over four years. In comparing alternative investments, people often use the "payback" method, which concentrates on the time period required to recoup the initial investment. In this case, the initial investment would be recouped in new assets from reinvestment of earnings and dividends in just over four years. This is an example of a low P/E-ratio stock.

On the other hand, if the investor wants to purchase high technology—high P/E-ratio stocks—he can buy Digital Equipment stock. This stock sells at $126, 2.19 times book value on December 31, 1982, and 18.37 times estimated earnings for 1983. Again, the Value Line Investment Survey is used for estimates and statistics.[16]

The company pays no dividend, and none is expected. Over the last five years, the return on equity has averaged 14½%. This is projected to be 13½% over the next several years. The earnings are expected to decline in 1983 to $6.85, but, even if normalized earnings are used, the stock still sells at 16.3 times estimated normalized earnings for 1983.

An investor in Digital Equipment stock at current prices is receiving an annuity of 6.1¢ that will compound at 13½%, the sustainable return on equity. The investor will have his $1.00 returned to him through earnings in 9.2 years, twice the time of R.J. Reynolds Industries stock.

Currently, high-grade intermediate corporate bonds yield 11%. Assuming that the coupons can be reinvested at 11%, an investor can double his money with bonds in 6.64 years. Given the alternative, an investor would be better off investing in bonds than in Digital Equipment stock, if his goal is to accumulate wealth rather than play the market.

[Authors note: This was written before the decline of Digital Equipment stock.]

References

1. David Dreman, *Contrarian Investment Strategy: The Psychology of Stock Market Success* (New York: Random House, 1979), p. 140.

2. Frank K. Reilly, *Investment Analysis and Portfolio Management* (Hinsdale, Ill.: Dryden Press, 1979), p. 281.

3. Michael E. Porter, *Competitive Strategy: Techniques For Analyzing Industries and Competitors* (New York: Free Press, 1980), p. 5.

4. George A. Christy and Peyton Foster Roden, Finance: *Environment and Decisions,* 2nd ed., Canfield Press, New York, 1976, p. 228.

5. Charles D. Ellis, "A Conversation With Benjamin Graham," *Financial Analysts Journal,* September-October 1976, p. 20.

6. Reilly, p. 37.

7. Sidney Homer and Martin L. Leibowitz, *Inside the Yield Book: New Tools for Bond Market Strategy* (Englewood Cliffs, N.J.: Prentice-Hall, 1972; New York: New York Institute of Finance, 1972) p. 31.

8. Leopold A. Bernstein, *Financial Statement Analysis: Theory, Application, and Interpretation,* The Willard J. Graham Series in Accounting, 1978 rev. ed. (Homewood, Ill.: Richard D. Irwin, 1978), p. 551.

9. Frank E. Block, "The Place of Book Value in Common Stock Evaluation," *Financial Analysts Journal,* March-April 1964, p. 29.

10. Guilford C. Babcock, "The Concept of Sustainable Growth" *Financial Analysts Journal,* May-June, 1979.

11. Warren E. Buffett, "How Inflation Swindles the Equity Investor," *Fortune Magazine,* Time, Inc., May, 1977, p. 250.

12. Mary Greenebaum, "Gauging the Market's Prospects," *Fortune Magazine,* ©Time, Inc. All rights reserved. January 10, 1983, p. 97.

13. Russell Fuller and Glenn H. Petry, "Inflation, Return on Equity and Stock Prices," *The Journal of Portfolio Management,* Summer 1981, pp. 19-20.

14. Homer & Leibowitz, p. 21.

15. Value Line Incorporated, *Value Line Investment Survey,* "Ratings & Reports," January 7, 1983, p. 334.

16. Value Line Incorporated, *Value Line Investment Survey,* "Ratings & Reports," November 12, 1982, p. 1098.

CHAPTER 4

Proof of Performance Over Time

Here is an expansion of the proof we offered in chapter 2 on the superior results of the low P/E-ratio investing method. Six of the most prominent researchers and practitioners of the low P/E-ratio philosophy are presented with their statistical studies and observations. The researchers' observations are important as they each add one more piece of knowledge to the low P/E-ratio approach to investing. The reader is presented with additional statistical evidence that low P/E-ratio investing does, in fact, result in superior investment performance.

The researchers can be divided into two major categories. Group A, those that pioneered in low P/E-ratio investing and Group B, those that built upon the theoretical foundations of Group A and are today's contemporary theoreticians and practitioners of the low P/E-ratio approach. Taken collectively, their studies and their experience span several generations.

Group A—the original group

The three most important researchers and/or practitioners in the original group are Benjamin Graham, S. Francis Nicholson, and Paul F. Miller.

Benjamin Graham—founder of the low P/E-ratio (or value) approach. Ben Graham, in the 1959 edition of *The Intelligent Investor*,[1] makes one of the first comparisons of low P/E-ratio versus high P/E-ratio investment programs. Graham took 30 Dow Jones stocks and made an evaluation of the 30 companies in relation to the December 1947 market prices on all 30 stocks. Of these stocks, Graham found three issues selling at more than the appraised value and five selling at two thirds of the appraised value. He then divided the 30 stocks into two groups: the "cheap" stocks, Group A; and the "dear" stocks, Group B.

Group A consisted of American Smelting & Refining, Goodyear Tire, Loew's Inc., Texas Company, and United Aircraft. Group B consisted of American Telephone & Telegraph, DuPont Chemical, and Johns-Manville. The appraisal in Table 4-1 shows the statistics for the two groups.

Table 4-1. Cheapest and dearest stocks.

	Group A	Group B
December 1947 price	$202.00	$379.00
Our appraised value	358.00	337.00
Tangible asset value	257.00	253.00
1947 Dividend	13.92	18.40
1947 Earnings.	42.75	20.29
1936-40 Earnings (average)	15.72	18.09
1929 Earnings.	25.23*	22.21
Future Earnings (Collins' estimate, p. 131)	31.16	25.92
Price-to-earnings ratio, 1947	4.7x	18.7x

* Excluding United Aircraft, formed in 1936.
Note: Appraisal values taken are without adjustment for assets.
Source: Graham, *The Intelligent Investor* (3rd ed.), p. 157.

The P/E ratios for the two groups were derived from the figures shown in Table 4-1 and added by the authors.

Graham then compares a $1,000 investment made in each group.

Table 4-2 shows what a $1,000 investment in each group would buy. Graham's appraised values and future earnings are forecasts or estimates; the remaining figures are actual values. The $1,000 investment purchased $1,290 of book value in Group A, with $69 in dividend income, a 6.9% yield. The $1,000 purchased $670 of book value in Group B, with $49 in dividend income, a 4.9% yield. The $1,000 investment purchased $214 of earnings in Group A for a 4.7 P/E multiple, while Group B purchased $54 of earnings for a P/E multiple of 18.7.

Table 4-2. Results per $1000 invested December 31, 1947.

	Group A	Group B	Ratio A/B
Appraised value	$1,760	$890	2.0 times
Asset value	1,290	670	1.9 times
1947 dividend....................	69	49	1.4 times
1947 earnings	214	54	4.0 times
1936-40 earnings	79	48	1.6 times
1929 earnings	146*	59	2.5 times
Future earnings (Collins' estimate)	155	69	2.3 times
Price-to-earnings ratio 1947	4.7x	18.7x	3.9 times

* On price of 4 issues.

Source: Graham, *The Intelligent Investor* (3rd ed.), p. 157.

Table 4-3 presents the results from the investments that were acquired in 1947 and then held through 1952.

Table 4-3. Performance of the "cheap group" vs. "dear group."

	"Cheap Group"	"Dear Group"	Dow-Jones Ind. Average
Price December 31, 1947	202.00	379.00	181.00
Our appraisal value	358.00	336.00	217.00
Price December 31, 1952	359.00	620.00	292.00
Dividends 1948-52	100.00	130.00	72.00
Over-all gain, Dec. 1947-Dec. 1952	257.00	371.00	183.00
Over-all gain, percent	127.00	98.00	101.00
Estimated earnings 1947-53 average....	29.20	19.20	14.95
Actual earnings 1947-52 average	42.06	33.89	24.81

Source: Graham, *The Intelligent Investor* (3rd ed.), p. 158.

When the dividend is added to the price at the end of 1952 and then compared to the price at the end of 1947, the "cheap group" did 30% better than the "dear group" and 27% better than the Dow Jones Industrial Averages. Table 4-4 shows the figures derived from Ben Graham's tables, reproduced above.

Table 4-4. Performance of groups vs. Dow-Jones.

	"Cheap Group"	"Dear Group"	Dow-Jones Ind. Average
Price, December 1952..............	359	620	292
Dividend........................	100	130	72
Total	459	750	364
Price, December 1947	202	379	181
Percent change...................	127	98	101

Source: Derived from Graham, *The Intelligent Investor* (3rd ed.).

In an updated study, presented in a later edition of *The Intelligent Investor,* Graham gives the performance results from 1952 through 1958. Graham's selection criteria were simplified by his choice of five stocks that have the lowest P/E multiples based on the previous year's earnings for the "cheap group" and five stocks that have the highest P/E multiples based on the previous year's earnings for the "dear group." Financial data for the "cheap group," "dear group," and a Dow Jones Unit for 1952 and 1958 are shown in Table 4-5.

Table 4-5. Performance of the "cheap and dear groups" (selected at Dec. 31, 1952).

	1952			1958		
	Cheap Group	Dear Group	D.–J. Unit	Cheap Group	Dear Group	D.–J. Unit
Price (Dec. 31)	244.00	327.00	292.00	714.00	628.00	584.00
Earnings	32.80	17.69	24.82	39.64	20.72	28.67
Price/earnings	7.4x	18.7x	11.8x	18.0x	30.3x	20.4x
Dividends	15.00	12.11	15.22	22.60	17.45	21.08
Dividend yield	6.15%	3.70%	5.21%	3.16%	2.78%	3.61%

"Cheap group": 1 share each of Amerian Smelting, Bethlehem Steel, Goodyear Tire, International Harvester, Texas Company.
"Dear group": 1 share each of Allied Chemical, American Can, DuPont, Eastman Kodak, Union Carbide.
Note: National Distillers was omitted from the "Dear Group" for special reasons and replaced by American Can. The substitution had no appreciable effect on the subsequent performance of the group.
Source: Graham, *The Intelligent Investor* (3rd ed.), p. 172.

Notice the P/E ratio of the groups in 1952 as well as their dividend yields. Once again, the low P/E-ratio stocks outperformed the high P/E-ratio stocks. The actual price performances of the groups are presented in Table 4-6.

Table 4-6. Performance of the "cheap and dear groups" (Selected at Dec. 31, 1952).

Increase: 1958 vs. 1952

	Cheap Group	Dear Group	D.–J. Unit
Price	193%	96%	100%
Over-all Gain*	240%	119%	143%
Earnings Rate	21%	17%	16%
Dividend Rate.	51%	44%	39%

* Based on price change plus dividends, 1953-58.

Source: Graham, *The Intelligent Investor* (3rd ed.), p. 171.

In this study, the "cheap group" outperformed the "dear group" and the Dow Jones 30 Industrials by 121% and 97%, respectively. Graham states:

> Studies we have made over the past ten years in the behavior of component issues in the Dow-Jones Industrial Unit have produced rather startling results. They suggest that for this particular group of 30 leading stocks the most effective method of selection may be the simplest—i.e., merely to pick out early each year the five which sell at the lowest multiplier of the previous year's earnings. Ever since 1932 this method would have yielded good comparative results, with only minor exceptions (Graham, p. 171).

In addition, Graham points out why it works:

> But the consistency with which similar performances have been made in other years covered by our studies indicates that there may here be an important principle at work. The principle would be that, on the whole, the stock market exaggerates its partialities and its prejudices, paying too much in the one case and too little in the other—especially when it is dealing with a group of large and powerful companies, such as are in the Dow-Jones list.
>
> *Not only that, but it appears that the market's forecasts of comparative earnings growth—as shown in high multipliers for some issues against low multipliers for others—are about as likely to be wrong as right* (Graham, p. 171).

Read it again. The authors can assure us, from their experience, that Graham's statement and excellent observation are absolutely true.

Graham provides further proof for the low P/E-ratio approach in a later revised *Intelligent Investor,* 1973 edition.[2] The study was done originally by Paul Miller when he was with Drexel & Company (see Table 4-7.)

Table 4-7. **Average annual percentage gain or loss on test issues, 1937-69.**

Period	10 Low-Multiplier Issues	10 High-Multiplier Issues	30 DJIA Stocks
1937-1942	− 2.2	− 10.0	− 6.3
1943-1947	17.3	8.3	14.9
1948-1952	16.4	4.6	9.9
1953-1957	20.9	10.0	13.7
1958-1962	10.2	− 3.3	3.6
1963-1969 (8 years) .	8.0	4.6	4.0

Source: Graham, *The Intelligent Investor* (4th ed.), p. 80.

That study will be discussed later in a section that covers Paul Miller's work. Graham refers to and discusses it in detail. Again, in this study, the low P/E-ratio group outperformed the high P/E-ratio group as well as outperforming the 30 Dow stocks.

One caveat to these findings was a late study, December 1968 to June 1971, done by Graham in preparation for his revised 1973 edition. Graham picked the low P/E-ratio stocks out of the Dow Jones Industrial Average first using six stocks, then using ten stocks. The results showed a below-average performance for the lower P/E-ratio stocks and an above-average performance for the higher P/E-ratio stocks. The sample was obviously very small, 30 stocks, but the findings disturbed him. His comment was:

> This one bad instance should not vitiate the conclusion based on 30-odd experiments, but its recent happenings gives it a special adverse weight. Perhaps the aggressive investor should start with the "low-multiplier" idea, but add other quantitative and qualitative requirements thereto in making up his portfolio (Graham, p. 82).

In Graham's articles and interviews, there is further proof for the low P/E-ratio philosophy. In a seminar, Charles D. Ellis, of Donaldson, Lufkin and Jenrette, interviewed Graham in a question-and-answer format. One of Graham's recommended approaches to investing was:

> . . . buying groups of stocks at less than their current or intrinsic value as indicated by one or more simple criteria. *The criterion I prefer is seven times the reported earnings for the past 12 months. You can use others—such as a current dividend return above seven percent or book value more than 120 percent of price,* etc. We are just finishing a performance study of these approaches over the past half-century—1925-75. They consistently show results of a 15 percent or better per annum, or twice the record of the DJIA for this long period. I have every confidence in the threefold merit of this general method based on (a) sound logic, (b) simplicity of application and (c) an excellent supporting record. *At bottom it is a technique by which true investors can exploit the recurrent excessive optimism and excessive apprehension of the speculative public.*[3]

This method of applying a simple criterion, such as seven (or less) times earnings for the past 12 months, consistently showed a 15% annual return in the studies made from 1925 through 1975, again proof of the low P/E-ratio approach.

Many have followed in Graham's footsteps and have offered additional proof of the benefit of using low P/E-ratios as the foundation of an investment program.

S. Francis Nicholson: challenging the status quo. Francis Nicholson, former vice-president of Provident Bank in Philadelphia, posed a question to himself and later to other professional investors. In "Price-Earnings Ratios" in the July-August 1960 issue of *Financial Analysts Journal,* Nicholson asked a question and stated his research findings:

> Within three to ten years, will the better price performance be in common stocks, with the current price earnings multiples of over 25 times, or in those under 12 times?
>
> Answers to this question as posed to sophisticated Financial Analysts and businessmen, in the past year, have been nearly ten-to-one in favor of the high multiples. It is assumed they are bought for growth, and the low multiples only for income.
>
> The results of certain studies, covering data for past years, would indicate a contrary conclusion, i.e., that on the average the purchase of stocks with low price-earnings multiples will result in greater ap-

preciation in addition to the higher income provided.[4]

At that time, and still today, Nicholson's conclusion was not accepted that low P/E-ratio stocks as a group outperform high P/E-ratio stocks. In this first study by Nicholson, 100 common stocks of trust quality were selected for the comparative study.

The period of the study covered 1939 to 1959. Prices and P/E ratios for 1939, 1944, 1949, 1954, and 1959 were gathered for each of the selected stocks. Utilities, banks, and finance and insurance companies were excluded. The stocks were divided into five groups by P/E ratio, and price appreciation was calculated, as shown in Table 4-8.

Table 4-8. Results of study #1: 100 stocks—Price appreciation in each period according to price-earnings groups.

Price-earnings ratios at beginning of each period	1939 1944	1939 1949	1939 1954	1939 1959	1944 1949	1944 1954	1944 1959	1949 1959	1949 1959	1954 1959	1957 1959
	%	%	%	%	%	%	%	%	%	%	%
Lowest 20 ratios	48	102	444	1,175	56	307	691	188	470	123	56
Next lowest 20	16	76	237	524	37	238	540	91	273	95	42
Middle 20	−5	25	114	329	36	152	570	122	328	88	40
Next highest 20	−4	18	140	378	26	100	305	84	291	79	26
Highest 20	5	43	206	542	33	156	508	51	273	115	39
Lowest 40	32	89	340	850	46	272	615	140	372	109	49
Middle 20	−5	25	114	329	36	152	570	122	328	88	40
Highest 40	1	29	169	457	30	128	406	68	282	97	33
Average for 100 stocks	12	53	228	589	38	191	523	107	327	100	40

Note: An inconsequential adjustment in the foregoing table was made in the periods beginning 1939 to omit four companies which had deficits or only nominal earnings.

Source: Nicholson, "Price-Earnings Ratio," p. 43.

As can be seen in Table 4-8, low P/E-ratio stocks outperformed high P/E-ratio stocks. Nicholson made several observations. The most noteworthy was:

If an investor bought the 20 lowest multiples in 1939, changed in 1944 to the 20 lowest in that year, and again in 1949 and 1954, his investment would have appreciated in 1959 to 14.7 times his original investment. Similar procedure with the 20 highest multiples in these years would have brought the value to 4.5 times the original investment. (These figures are of course not adjusted for broker commissions and taxes.)(Nicholson, p. 44.)

Nicholson also ran a study on the chemical industry, 29 stocks, and produced similar results, as shown in Table 4-9.

Table 4-9. Results: lowest and highest multiples.

At the beginning of each 3-, 6-, or 10-year period	3-Yr. Average Appreciation From Each Year 1937-1954 Inclusive	6-Yr. Average Appreciation From Each Year 1937-1951 Inclusive	10-Yr. Average Appreciation From Each Year 1937-1947 Inclusive
5 stocks with highest P/E ratios ...	21%	50%	116%
5 stocks with lowest P/E ratios	56%	101%	191%
Highest 50% P/E ratios	24%	54%	109%
Lowest 50% P/E ratios	40%	89%	153%
Total number of years covered	18	15	11
Number of years in which average appreciation was higher			
in the highest 50% ratios	2	3	3
in the lowest 50% ratios	16	12	8

Source: Nicholson, "Price-Earnings Ratio," p. 44.

Again low P/E-ratio stocks outperformed high P/E-ratio stocks. Nicholson's conclusion from the 1960 *Financial Analysts Journal* article was:

> These studies seem to confirm that present or immediately prospective earnings are a major factor in the outlook for market prices of common stocks. Many investors have apparently underestimated the importance of reasonable price-earnings relationships. High price-earnings multiples typically reflect investor satisfaction with companies of high quality, or with those which have experienced several years of expansion and rising earnings. A resultant increase in price-earnings ratios may be justified in individual instances, but under the impact of public approval or even glamour, it often runs

to extremes. When this occurs, upward price trends are eventually subject to slow-down or reversal. High multiple stocks then develop trends which on the average compare unfavorably with low multiple stocks which have not yet been bid up to vulnerable price levels.

Some growth stocks appear to be exceptions, at least for temporary periods, and in individual instances price advances have continued spectacularly. These exceptions may explain why investors do not look on high price-earnings ratios as danger signals but, on the contrary, regard them as evidence of potential growth and of further price appreciation to be expected. The results of our studies cast doubt on the validity of such reasoning and point up the relative risks of buying stocks after prices have advanced beyond conservative price-earnings relationships (Nicholson, p. 45).

But a problem arose. Nicholson was challenged seven years later by Nicholas Molodovsky in an article, "Recent Studies of P/E Ratios," in the May-June 1967 issue of *Financial Analysts Journal.* Molodovsky's two basic objections were,

1. Nicholson's Study #2 on the chemical industry was flawed because the sample was too small; and (paraphrasing Cootner's article)
2. Paul H. Cootner in an article published in the *Commercial & Financial Chronicle* of September 16, 1965, said,

All his 100 stocks were high grade; they had been selected from the vantage point of that year. His selections might have been quite different if they had been made at the beginning of the entire period, i.e., in 1939. Many of such stocks would possibly no longer have been in Nicholson's 1960 sample by losing, in the meantime, their high investment rating, and thus dropping out. Dr. Cootner thought that, if there is a fallacy in Mr. Nicholson's results, it is likely to arise from the use of hindsight in determining what is a high-grade stock.[5]

The questions and concerns were legitimate, but Nicholson retaliated the following year with his widely quoted article, "Price Ratios in Relation to Investment Results."

In recent years, several studies have been publicized with respect to the superior average price-performance of stocks with low price earnings ratios. The literature of this subject was reviewed comprehensively in the May-June *Financial Analysts Journal* by Nicholas

Molodovsky. . . . I agree that security analysis procedures may properly involve these and many other areas of inquiry but the significance of price ratios in relation to investment performance requires dealing with actual figures rather than any form of adjusted data. The purpose of studying the significance of price ratios is not accomplished by concluding in advance that they are of doubtful value unless other data is substituted. . .(Nicholson, p. 105).

Nicholson accepted Molodovsky's criticisms and said that he looked forward to a much more detailed study which he then proceeded to present.

This is Nicholson's most quoted study on P/E ratios. Tables 4-10 and 4-11 show the results, together with Nicholson's comments. The study period covers 1937 through 1962.

Table 4-10. Annual earnings related to mean prices.

Grouped According to Quintiles in Each Year, 1937 to 1962 Inclusive	After	Average Price Appreciation Percentages						
		1 yr. %	2 yr. %	3 yr. %	4 yr. %	5 yr. %	6 yr. %	7 yr. %
A Lowest price-earnings ratios . . .		16	34	55	76	98	125	149
B Next higher		9	22	34	48	65	82	100
C Next higher		7	18	30	43	60	77	96
D Next higher		6	14	24	35	50	65	83
E Highest price-earnings		3	11	21	31	46	65	84

Comment: With the large number of items and periods averaged above, the pattern of price changes seems remarkably consistent.

Note: The performance of the A group after four years was best in 22 out of 23 years. The worst performance after four years occurred in the E group in 13 years and in the D group in 6 years.

Source: Nicholson, "Price Ratios in Relation to Investment Result," p. 106.

The format for the study was,
1. The 189 companies in 18 industries that were included were mostly the larger and more important companies in their respective industries.
2. No bank, insurance, utility, or transportation stocks were included.

Table 4-11. Annual earnings related to mean prices.

Grouped Each Year 1937-1962 Inclusive by Fixed Ranges	Number of Cases averaged	Average Price Appreciation Percentages						
		After 1 yr. %	2 yr. %	3 yr. %	4 yr. %	5 yr. %	6 yr. %	7 yr. %
A 10 times or less	1672 to 1582	13	31	51	71	90	110	131
B 10 to 12 times	662 to 525	8	19	31	41	50	68	87
C 12 to 15 times	872 to 606	6	15	24	36	52	70	88
D 15 to 20 times	773 to 457	4	11	18	26	40	55	75
E Over 20 times	581 to 277	2	4	10	17	32	54	71

Comment: It is evident that differences in performance are accentuated when the categories are based on fixed price-earnings ranges rather than on quintiles. The differences shown above are not caused by a few unusually high or low figures. An actual count of items involved in Table 4-11 shows price performance after five years as follows:

Percentages of Total Number of Items

	With Price Gains 100% or More	With Losses
A Group	37.0%	10.6%
B Group	19.8	19.1
C Group	18.4	22.2
D Group	16.0	30.5
E Group	10.6	35.2

Source: Nicholson, "Price Ratios in Relation to Investment Results," p. 106.

3. No industries were included unless data were available for at least four companies in each industry. Otherwise, all companies in the industry summaries received from Studley Shubert & Co. were included in this study without any attempt to influence the composition of the list toward any prejudged criteria. The list was by no means limited to companies with recent records of successful operation from the standpoint of an investor.

4. Percentage price changes, based on mean prices, were calculated for each year in the 1937-63 period. Such price changes were for periods of one, two, three, four, five, six, and seven years after each base year, or about 28,000 price calculations. Average prices

were used since the available data was on this basis, but it is believed that the comparative results would not have been significantly different if prices had been used for a particular date in each year.

5. For each year, per-share data was tabulated for earnings, non-cash charges, hereafter referred to as depreciation, sales, and book value. Ratios of these data to prices were computed for each stock for each year for which figures were available, except that earnings ratios were not included when prices were more than 50 times earnings or when there were no earnings.

6. Price ratios for each year were grouped on a graduated basis and averages were calculated for the highest, the lowest and the three in-between groups. Averages were then computed for all years to give an over-all picture of relative performance.

7. Because the basic study ended with the 1963 figures, further calculations were made of relative price changes from the years 1959, 1960, 1961, 1962, and 1963 to November 1, 1966, as a means of bringing the study up-to-date for recent periods.

Again, low P/E-ratio stocks outperformed high P/E-ratio stocks. Additionally, Nicholson brings the study further up-to-date by running an additional study from 1959, 1960, 1961, 1962, and 1963 to November 1, 1966.

Again these were the same results. Low P/E-ratio stocks outperformed high P/E-ratio stocks. Nicholson compared prices to other factors such as sales, depreciation charges, and book value and found the relationship of "getting more for your money" also rewarding. In fact, one study on price-to-book value relationships shown in Table 4-13 will have significant meaning farther on in chapter 3.

The book-value study shows that the higher book value one has for the price he pays, the better the performance. Nicholson closed,

In conclusion—what does this study mean? A quick answer is that the comparative figures in this report speak for themselves. If, for example, about 4,000 calculations of price changes over a quarter century show five-year appreciation averaging 32% for those stocks with price-earnings ratios over 20 times and 90% for those with ratios of 10 times or less, there is a clear inference that high earnings figures are desirable and that low earnings are a basis for questioning. This inference is strengthened by the comparisons of average appreciation over longer periods of 6 and 7 years and shorter periods of 1 to 4 years. It is logical that purchasers seek the most for their

Table 4-12. Calculations for periods ending November 1, 1966.

As a means of bringing the study nearer the present date, calculations of price changes were made to November 1, 1966, from the mean prices of 1959, 1960, 1961, 1962, and 1963, respectively, making a total of 905 such calculations for a total of 181 stocks. These were grouped for the purpose of comparative price performance according to the categories already used in this report with the following results:

	Average Appreciation to 11/1/66 as Defined Above	Per Cent of Total Number Showing 50% or More Appreciation	Percent of Total Number Showing Any Losses
A and B — Under 12 times	72%	60%	21%
C — 12 to 15 times	38	32	33
D — 15 to 20 times	18	19	39
E — Over 20 times	13	17	51

Comment: The definitions of the group categories in Table 4-11 are the same as in Table 10 except that the A and B groups are combined. The price performance patterns are not entirely the same as those shown in previous tables, but it seems clear that most of the data above for the various D and E groups indicate below-average results and most of the data for the combined A and B groups indicate relatively superior results, despite a number of A items with poor results. In observing statistical patterns such as those in Table 4-12 and also in previous tables, it should, of course, be noted that the records of individual stocks and of industry groups often differ widely.

Source: Nicholson, "Price Ratios in Relation to Investment Results," p. 109.

money, and the purchaser of common stocks may logically seek the greater productivity represented by stocks with low rather than high price earnings ratios. Also, in seeking the most for his money, the purchaser of common stocks may reasonably conclude that there are plus factors in his favor if depreciation reserves are substantial rather than minimal. Emphasis on these factors does not preclude him from endeavoring to recognize any situations with good prospects including those relatively rare growth stocks whose prices do not yet reflect all or most of expected future benefits. He is likely to have better than average results from reliance on good current figures. If good current figures and growth prospects can be combined, these are even better opportunities for successful investment.

Table 4-13. Annual book value related to mean prices.

Grouped According to Quintiles in Each Year, 1937 to 1962 Inclusive	Average Price Appreciation Percentages after 1 yr. %	2 yr. %	3 yr. %	4 yr. %	5 yr. %	6 yr. %	7 yr. %
A Lowest price-book value ratio......	9	24	41	59	81	107	132
B Next higher....................	9	22	36	51	67	85	105
C Next higher	8	17	28	41	56	73	91
D Next higher	7	16	27	38	53	70	87
E Highest price-book value ratio	9	19	31	45	62	80	101

Comment: No significant differences appear in the 1st year, and thereafter the differences are less pronounced than in earlier tables. The best four-year performance was registered in 11 years for the A group, three years for the B group, no years for the C group, two years for the D group and seven years for the E group. The corresponding numbers of years of worst four-year performance were 0, 3, 6, 7, and 7 for these groups, respectively.

Source: Nicholson, "Price Ratios in Relation to Investment Results," p. 108.

Table 4-14. Annual book value related to mean prices.

Grouped Each Year 1937-1962 Inclusive by Fixed Ranges Book Value % of Price	Number of Cases Averaged	Average Price Appreciation Percentages after 1 yr. %	2 yr. %	3 yr. %	4 yr. %	5 yr. %	6 yr. %	7 yr. %
A Over 150%	691 to 602	13	32	54	77	99	124	149
B 100% to 150%	879 to 682	9	24	39	53	70	91	112
C 60% to 100%	1558 to 1188	7	16	26	39	55	72	91
D 30% to 60%	1225 to 876	6	15	26	39	54	71	90
E Under 30%	288 to 162	5	11	19	29	46	67	86

Comment: With the fixed ranges above, the price performance differences are much more pronounced. Despite wide differences in character of assets, historical factors and profit margins, it would appear that, on the average, high book value in relation to price is a factor associated with relatively favorable price performance.

Source: Nicholson, "Price Ratios in Relation to Investment Results," p. 108.

In Further Conclusion—What is the Significance of Price Ratios in Security Analysis?

The real value of price ratios is to use corporate figures as a guide to determine whether stock prices are high or low. Successful investment depends in large measure on the ability to determine the price ranges within which stocks may be advantageously bought or sold. Suppose for example, a stock appreciated from a mean price of 50 in 1964 to a current price of 75 in 1967 or a 50% gain. Assuming a price range within 1964 of 40 to 60, a purchaser at 40 or 45 would have an 87½ or 66⅔% gain in 1967 whereas a purchaser at 55 or 60 would have only a 36% or 25% gain. The sharp contrasts in these figures illustrate the reason for paying attention to price ratios or to any other evidence that prices are high or low relative to their intrinsic value or relative to the prices of other stocks. This attention to stock prices and price ratios may have a greater effect on investment performance than much of the effort devoted to fine distinctions concerning growth estimates or the determination of blue chip qualifications.

Price earnings ratios are usually shown in analytical reports but in many cases of 20 to 50 times earnings, the ratios are assumed to be normal with no word of caution... Should not the investor know, for example, whether assets and sales are approximately 25% or 125% of his investment dollar and whether depreciation charges are a trivial ½% or a substantial 8½% of the cost of his investment?... (Nicholson, pp. 108-109).

Paul F. Miller, Jr., persistently looking at the facts. Paul Miller was vice-president of Drexel, Harriman & Ripley, originally the Drexel Co., when he did several studies on P/E ratios to determine whether P/E ratio rankings had any relationship to price performance. The first study, released in the Drexel & Co., Philadelphia, October 1966, monthly review,[7] is reflected in Table 4-15.
     This study shows low P/E-ratio stocks outperforming high P/E-ratio stocks.
     In September 1966, Miller and Ernest R. Widmann, an economist at Drexel & Co., wrote an article for *The Commercial and Financial Chronicle* entitled "Price Performance Outlook for High & Low P/E-ratio stocks." In this paper they described their above mentioned study, Table 4-15, of the high and low P/E-ratio stocks. They took data for the period from 1948 through 1964 from

Table 4-15. Average price increase per year, 1948-64.

P/E Quintile	Price Increase
1st (highest P/E)	7.7%
2nd	9.2
3rd	12.0
4th	12.8
5th (Lowest P/E)	18.4

Source: Miller, "Drexel & Co. Monthly Review," October 1966.

the Compustat 1800 Industrial Tapes with the following characteristics:
1. The company had to be an industrial company.
2. The sales had to be over $150 million.
3. The fiscal year had to run from September 30 to January 31.
4. Companies with zero or negative earnings were excluded.

"Price-earnings Ratios were computed using year-end prices and fiscal year earnings. The price performance of the qualifying companies were computed for all one-year periods following the year-end price-earnings ratio calculations. Then an average price performance was computed for each P/E quintile."[8]

As the years went by from 1948 through 1964, the number of companies qualifying went from 110 to 334. Table 4-15 is self-explanatory. As we stated, low P/E-ratio stocks outperformed high P/E-ratio stocks.

Miller and Widmann also described the consistency of the results in the following tables.

Table 4-16. Performance of stocks ranked in quintiles by P/E at each year-end during 17 subsequent one-year periods (1948-64 inclusive).

P/E Quintile	Number of Years in Which Price Performance Ranked				
	First	Second	Third	Fourth	Fifth
First (High P/E)	1	3	2	3	8
Second	1	1	2	11	2
Third	1	5	7	1	3
Fourth	2	7	4	2	2
Fifth (Low P/E)	12	1	2	0	2

Source: Miller and Widmann, "Price Performance Outlook," p. 26.

Table 4-17. Performance over 15 three-year periods.

P/E Quintile	Number of Years in Which Price Performance Ranked				
	First	Second	Third	Fourth	Fifth
First (High P/E)	2	1	1	2	9
Second	0	1	0	10	4
Third	1	3	8	2	1
Fourth	2	8	3	1	1
Fifth (Low P/E)	10	2	3	0	0

Source: Miller and Widmann, "Price Performance Outlook," p. 76.

Table 4-18. Performance over 13 five-year periods.

P/E Quintile	Number of Years in Which Price Performance Ranked				
	First	Second	Third	Fourth	Fifth
First (High P/E)	2	2	0	1	8
Second	0	4	1	5	3
Third	0	0	9	2	2
Fourth	1	6	3	3	0
Fifth (Low P/E)	10	1	0	2	0

Source: Miller and Widmann, "Price Performance Outlook," p. 26.

In the one-year studies, low P/E-ratio stocks outperformed the other groups in 12 out of 17 instances; in the three-year-period study, 10 out of 15 occurrences, and in the five-year-period study, 10 out of 13 occurrences. This study shows the consistency of the above-average performance of the low P/E-ratio stock group.

In addition, Miller and Widmann axcertained that, "The better performance of the low P/E group is *not* caused by a few stocks making unusually large gains and offsetting the dismal performance of the majority of the stocks in this group" (Miller and Widmann, p. 27).

Another study that Miller did, and that Widmann and others worked on with him, was the study done on the 30 Dow Jones Industrial Stocks. This study is more widely known, because it is reported in Graham's revised edition of the *Intelligent Investor*.[9]

Table 4-19. Average annual percentage gain or loss on test issues, 1937-69.

Period	10 Low-Multiple Issues	10 High-Multiple Issues	30 DJIA Stocks
1937-42...............	− 2.2	− 10.0	− 6.3
1943-47...............	17.3	8.3	14.9
1948-52...............	16.4	4.6	9.9
1953-57...............	20.9	10.0	13.7
1958-62...............	10.2	− 3.3	3.6
1963-69...............	8.0	4.6	4.0

Source: Graham, *The Intelligent Investor* (4th ed.), p. 80.

Thirty stocks are not statistically significant to prove a point about low or high P/E-ratio stocks, but this early attempt led to more complicated studies. Miller and Widmann continued to update the original work. As can be seen, the 10 low-multiple stock issues outperformed the 10 high-multiple stock issues and the Dow 30 stocks in total.

Miller and Widmann had more to say, outside the scope of this chapter, about why the low P/E-ratio stocks outperformed the high P/E-ratio stocks. The reader is encouraged to read the quoted article to understand their reasoning.[8]

Group B—contemporary researchers or practitioners

The five most prominent contemporary researchers or practitioners are David Dreman; W. Anthony Hitschler and Benedict E. Capaldi, Jr.; and John W. Peavy, III, and David A. Goodman.

David Dreman, leader of the second generation. David Dreman, president of Dreman, Gray and Embry, Inc., an investment counseling firm, is the modern-day proponent of low P/E-ratio investing. Dreman has written two investment classics, *Psychology and the Stock Market,* in 1976, and *Contrarian Investment Strategy,* in 1979.[10] *Barrons* has stated, in its book review section, that Dreman's *Contrarian Investment Strategy is possibly the most important investment book to be published since Graham's Security Analysis.*

Dreman has covered some of the historical work on low P/E-ratio investing and continues to receive new work done by others. Dreman's statistical work, revealed in his book and in several articles, continues to prove the low P/E-ratio philosophy.

Four major studies done by Dreman add proof of the superiority of low P/E-ratio investing. Dreman used the Compustat 1800 industrial tapes. Included in the sample of 1,251 issues were 70% of the common stocks listed on the New York Stock Exchange as well as large companies on the American Stock Exchange and over-the-counter markets. The requirements were:

1. Fiscal years must end in March, June, September, or December.
2. In the high P/E-ratio group, a maximum P/E multiple of 75 was used to eliminate companies with minimal earnings.
3. Hindsight bias was removed. This was a criticism of one of Nicholson's earlier studies.
4. Year-end earnings, or the most recent twelve-month earnings to the end of each period, were used along with prices on the last day of trading two months later. Thus, the earnings information was fully public at the time, and the P/E ratios were currently available in financial publications.

Given this information, Dreman conducted four studies covering different

Table 4-20. Anualized compound rates of return, August 1968-August 1977 (full period of study).

Stocks Ranked by P/E Multiples Decile*	Switching Stocks After Each				Holding Original Portfolio for 9 Years
	1 Quarter	6 Months	1 Year	3 Years	
1 (highest)	− 2.64%	− 1.06%	− 1.13%	− 1.43%	0.33%
2	0.92	1.62	0.56	− 0.28	1.27
3	0.51	0.62	1.63	0.85	3.30
4	3.06	3.42	3.31	4.87	5.36
5	2.19	4.46	2.93	5.02	3.72
6	4.84	5.33	6.70	4.82	4.52
7	7.90	6.07	6.85	5.89	6.08
8	8.83	8.24	8.56	7.78	6.35
9	11.85	8.40	6.08	7.73	6.40
10 (lowest)	14.00	11.68	10.26	10.89	7.89

Average return of sample. 4.75%

* Take all stocks in study and divide them into ten groups according to the price to earnings multiple.
Source: Dreman, *Contrarian Investment Strategy*, p. 131.

market periods. The first study, shown in Table 4-20, ran from August 1968, to August 1977.

Switching stocks quarterly showed the best results, but, even if the portfolio were held for the full nine-year period, the results were much above average for the low P/E-ratio groups and below average for the high P/E-ratio groups.

The results become even more vivid when they are converted into dollars and are compounded at the rates of return shown in Table 4-20. Table 4-21 summarizes.

The second study covered the May 1970 to November 1974 market. This is from a market bottom to a market bottom. Table 4-22 shows the results.

Again the low P/E-ratio stocks outperformed the high P/E-ratio stocks by a wide margin. Over the four-and-one-half-year period, low P/E-stock prices with dividends added compounded at 2.27% per year while the high P/E-ratio group's price with dividends added *declined* at 1.54% per year. All the results were poor, but the low P/E-ratio stocks performed much better than the whole group. Why the poor performance from the bottom of the 1970 market to the bottom of the 1974 market? The reason: the bottom of the 1974 market was lower than the bottom of the 1970 market for all indexes, especially the Value Line Composite and the Standard & Poor's 500.

Table 4-21. Results—nine-year period.

	Performance: Switching Quarterly	
	August 1968	August 1977
Lowest P/E ratio decile . . .	$10,000	$32,519
Highest P/E ratio decile . .	$10,000	$ 7,708
	Performance: Switching Yearly	
	August 1968	August 1977
Lowest P/E ratio decile . . .	$10,000	$24,086
Highest P/E ratio decile . .	$10,000	$ 9,038
	Performance: Holding for Full 9 Years	
	August 1968	August 1977
Lowest P/E ratio decile . . .	$10,000	$19,824
Highest P/E ratio decile . .	$10,000	$10,306

Source: Bowen and Ganucheau.

Table 4-22. Annualized compound rates of return, May 1970-November 1974 (market bottom to bottom).

Stocks Ranked by P/E Multiples Decile	1 Quarter	Switching After Each 6 Months	9 Months	2¼ Years	Holding Original Portfolio for 4½ Years
1 (highest)	−5.45%	−5.08%	−2.67%	−5.33%	−1.54%
2	0.68	0.80	0.59	−6.07	−0.98
3	−2.64	−0.99	−1.91	−2.84	−2.49
4	−1.52	−3.02	−0.82	−2.47	−0.73
5	−4.05	−2.84	−2.39	−2.02	−0.89
6	−1.74	0.87	−0.60	−1.78	−1.80
7	2.34	1.34	0.55	1.52	1.21
8	0.85	0.17	−0.35	4.04	3.32
9	2.00	1.50	−1.04	0.88	−0.65
10 (lowest)	6.01	3.12	2.54	5.04	2.27
Average return of sample............−0.60%					

Source: Dreman, *Contrarian Investment Strategy*, p. 132.

The third study, covering the period from the bottom of the market in the 1970 correction to the top of the recovery market in 1976, ran from August 1970 through August 1976. Table 4-23 below shows the results.

Again, there was a superior performance for the low P/E-ratio groups. Whether switching annually or holding the original portfolio, the group with low P/E-ratio stocks outperformed the group with high P/E-ratio stocks.

The fourth study covers the great "two-tier-market" that occurred between May 1970 and February 1973. This period was characterized by the thought that high P/E-ratio companies deserved their multiples because they had the ability to continue to increase their earnings at above-average rates because of pricing flexibility. This was the era of "one-decision stocks," or the "nifty 50," buy-and-hold-forever regardless of the P/E multiple. Table 4-24 shows the results.

Table 4-23. Annualized compound rates of return, August 1970-August 1976.

Stocks Ranked by P/E Multiples Decile	Switching After Each:			Holding Original Portfolio for:		
	1 Year	2 Years	3 Years	4 Years	5 Years	6 Years
1 (highest)	6.10%	4.93%	3.50%	−1.45%	5.07%	7.07%
2	6.25	2.48	5.64	−1.42	6.47	8.03
3	8.01	6.72	10.07	−2.49	4.68	8.20
4	8.79	7.60	8.14	−4.95	3.33	7.26
5	7.49	9.52	12.00	−3.42	4.73	9.91
6	11.99	10.91	10.67	−2.81	5.58	9.91
7	12.36	13.28	11.67	1.21	7.69	11.99
8	12.79	12.70	11.64	−0.82	6.34	11.41
9	8.61	11.16	11.50	1.47	7.19	12.30
10 (lowest)	14.13	15.45	15.16	0.09	7.66	12.39

Source: Dreman, *Contrarian Investment Strategy*, p. 134.

Table 4-24. Annualized compound rates of return, May 1970-February 1973 (two-tier market).

Stocks Ranked by P/E Multiples Decile	Switching After Each:				Holding Original Portfolio for:
	1 Quarter	6 Months	1 Year	2 Years	2¾ Years
1 (highest)	13.07%	12.51%	15.78%	12.84%	12.40%
2	19.19	20.66	15.05	12.04	13.01
3	14.11	15.49	17.64	16.17	15.86
4	13.95	13.27	14.34	13.12	14.97
5	10.71	10.56	12.66	13.32	16.94
6	13.19	15.88	15.75	12.22	12.98
7	14.83	14.26	13.10	15.39	16.01
8	15.06	14.54	14.19	16.93	17.23
9	16.45	17.83	17.56	19.36	14.20
10 (lowest)	20.35	16.09	15.41	18.56	15.25

Average return of sample. 14.54%

Source: Dreman, *Contrarian Investment Strategy*, p. 134.

In a period when institutions were all doing the same thing, that is, buying the one-decision stocks, the low P/E-ratio group outperformed again except for the one-year holding period. In comparison to the low P/E-ratio stocks, the high P/E-ratio stocks did better in this study period than in any study period before. They still did not outperform the low P/E-ratio stocks except for the one-year holding period. The remarkable thing is that this was a period when almost everyone believed that the high P/E-ratio group was the group to own.

Dreman sums up,

> The findings presented here certainly make it appear that the advantage of a low P/E stragegy is clearcut. In our work, it did not matter whether the investor started near a market top or a market bottom; superior returns were provided in any phase of the market cycle (including the top-tier mania). And the cycle we measured showed the widest fluctuations of any in the postwar period. The average multiple of the S & P 425 varied sharply—from a high of 21 to a low of 7—yet the findings consistently and dramatically supported the strategy of buying and holding out-of-favor stocks. The results in the study were certainly more striking than I had expected. If anything, they indicated patterns of investor behavior—and error— far more systematic than one would have believed possible (Dreman, pp. 133-135).

Dreman, with his four studies as well as other studies and insights into the psychological reasons why the low P/E-ratio strategy works, carries the banner from the previous generation in Group A. Any serious student of low P/E-ratio investing must read both of Dreman's books. The presentation here has merely scratched the surface.

W. Anthony Hitschler and Benedict E. Capaldi, Jr., picking up where Nicholson left off at Provident. W. Anthony Hitschler is president of Provident Capital Management, a subsidiary of the Provident Bank in Philadelphia. Hitschler continues a long line of proponents of low P/E-ratio investing at Provident beginning with Francis S. Nicholson.

In an article titled, "To Know What We Don't Know or the Caribou Wasn't in the Estimates," January-February 1980 *Financial Analyst Journal,* Hitschler outlines the reasons for the low P/E-ratio strategy.[11] He shows the fallacy of relying on analysts' estimates for investment decisions and then presents Nicholson's 1937-62 study showing the superior returns for low P/E-ratio stocks.

The unique factors in Hitschler's further studies are, first, the updated studies running from December 1958 through December 1978 on the low P/E-ratio stocks versus the high P/E-ratio stocks; second, on the same group divided by the return on equity; and third, the comments on the historical degree of P/E multiple compression between the five P/E-ratio groups.

In Hitschler's 1958-78 study, he set out to update the performance for the five P/E-ratio groups and to see if there was a consistent effect on stock returns caused by return-on-equity. Table 4-25 shows the results.[12]

Hitschler's studies for the 20-year period again prove the validity of the low P/E-ratio approach to investing. The low P/E-ratio stocks across all levels of return-on-equity provide superior returns whether the sample has been weighted—large and small firms lumped together—or unweighted, that is, equal dollar investment in large and small firms.

The study presents evidence that there is no correlation between return-on-equity and levels of returns. Hitschler says that the return-on-equity factor is

Table 4-25. Annual compound rate of growth with dividend reinvestment (Study Results from 12/1958 through 12/1978).

(A) *Unweighted*

			Return on Equity			
	Low ROE	2 ROE	3 ROE	4 ROE	High ROE	Avg.
Low P/E Quintile	22.9	21.6	18.5	19.5	30.1	22.7
2 P/E	16.6	12.9	12.9	14.8	15.5	14.7
3 P/E	12.6	8.0	8.6	10.9	13.2	10.6
4 P/E	9.6	4.0	3.5	6.9	12.8	7.7
High P/E	9.7	1.5	5.0	6.2	11.5	7.9
Average	13.4	10.8	10.1	12.0	17.5	12.8

(B) *Weighted*

			Return on Equity			
	Low ROE	2 ROE	3 ROE	4 ROE	High ROE	Avg.
Low P/E Quintile	16.6	14.7	14.8	12.6	16.8	14.3
2 P/E	11.9	11.0	11.2	8.2	9.8	9.5
3 P/E	10.0	8.9	6.0	6.5	9.0	8.3
4 P/E	5.5	2.6	4.5	5.9	5.5	4.7
High P/E	2.9	− 1.9	3.5	4.4	7.0	4.9
Average	6.9	6.2	6.6	5.8	8.1	6.7

Source: Hitschler, "Study Results."

driven by an improving return-on-equity or a declining return-on-equity. He says that the best of both worlds is a low P/E-ratio stock with an improving return-on-equity.

The third unique factor in Hitschler's studies is the comment on the historical degree of P/E multiple compression between the five P/E ratio groups. Adversaries had been saying that the low P/E ratio effect would not continue to work because of the tremendous compression of the five P/E ratio groups over the past several years. In his 1980 article, Hitschler says,

> Provident Capital Management has attempted to measure the degree of P/E multiple compression that has occurred over the last 20 years. Our preliminary conclusion is that the present level of P/E dispersion is in the middle of the historical range.

> As of the year-end 1958, for example, the median P/E of the highest quintile was 31 percent above the median P/E of the universe, and that of the lowest quintile was, coincidentially, 31 percent below the median multiple. Twenty years later, the top quintile was 33 percent above and the lowest quintile 27 percent below the middle. In contrast to 1973, when the median P/E of the top quintile reached 113 percent of the median P/E of the universe, the *present degree* of dispersion of P/E multiples is similar to the dispersion that existed 20 years ago. During the intervening 20 years, the lowest P/E group provided the best return in 14 years, versus three for the highest P/E group (Hitschler, p. 31).

In a follow-up article, Hitschler says that, with the unusually good performance of the high P/E-ratio group in 1980, the multiple discrepancy between low P/E-ratio stocks and high P/E-ratio stocks is almost back to its old high for the last 22 years. Conversely, the discount on the fourth and fifth P/E-ratio quintiles is now near the maximum of the range for 22 years, suggesting that low P/E-ratio stocks are likely to provide unusually good returns for the next year or so.

Hitschler also updated the figures to 1978, challenged us on the effect of return-on-equity, and introduced a new concept of relative compression of multiple groups. This compression of multiple groups will be studied later by Benedict E. Capaldi, who also is a vice-president at Provident Capital Management.

Hitschler, like Dreman, is involved in active professional money management, using the low P/E-ratio approach. Their mastery of this concept is apparent in their performance figures and in their success in building their organizations.

Benedict E. Capaldi, Jr., tries to optimize returns from low P/E-ratio investing by correlating with economic cycles. Ben Capaldi is employed at Provident Capital Management with Hitschler. Earlier we showed how Hitschler studied the compression of P/E multiples among the five P/E-ratio groups to determine if there were certain times when the low P/E-ratio group's performance would vary from the norm. Hitschler concluded by saying that the two lowest P/E-ratio quintiles were unusually depressed in relation to the highest P/E-ratio quintile; therefore, the low P/E ratio quintile should have done very well over the succeeding year, 1980-81.

Capaldi's contribution was an attempt to do as Hitschler has done, i.e., to see if there are special times when low P/E-ratio stocks do better or worse than the market. Capaldi, however, used economic cycles in an article for *Pensions & Investment Age,* December 6, 1982, titled "Low P/E's: Optimal Investing." Capaldi says,

> The purpose of this brief study is to examine the 'behavioral pattern' of low P/E stocks during various phases of the economic cycle. In doing this we should be able to determine an optimal timing strategy for low P/E investment.[13]

First, Capaldi updated, through June 1982 the Provident low P/E-ratio study by Hitschler referred to earlier.

Table 4-26. Annual compound rates of growth with dividend reinvested (study results from December 12, 1958 through May 6, 1982).

	Yearly Rate of Return
Low P/E Quintile	15.4%
2 P/E Quintile	11.1%
3 P/E Quintile	9.5%
4 P/E Quintile	6.0%
High P/E Quintile	6.1%
S&P 500 Index	7.5%

Source: Capaldi, "Low P/Es: Optimal Investing," p. 23.

The low P/E-ratio philosophy continued to prove itself over the long term.

Second, Capaldi analyzed the pattern of low P/E-ratio returns generated during the six economic cycles within the period of the study, 1959-66/1982. The low P/E-ratio group outperformed both the Standard & Poor's 500 and the high P/E-ratio group 16 of 23 times. On an equally weighted basis, the low P/E-ratio group outperformed the Standard & Poor's 500 19 of 23 times.

Capaldi stated that the most interesting periods are when the low P/E-ratio group has turned in a subpar performance. According to Capaldi's studies, five of the seven times that low P/E-ratio stocks underperformed the Standard & Poor's 500, or high P/E-ratio stocks, were during times of "clearly defined recessions or economic slowdowns" (p.23). Capaldi states:

> It is fairly obvious from the graph that the worst relative returns are generated going into and during the early phases of the economic slowdown. It is just as evident that as the recession abates and the market recovers, the rates of return achieved by the low P/E groups substantially exceed those of the S&P 500 as well as the returns of the high P/E group.

> These excess returns appear to be achieved for as long as the economic recovery remains visible (p. 23).

But why?

> The most reasonable explanation for the consistent behavioral difference between the returns of the two P/E groups is that low P/E stocks are more closely related to general economic activity while high P/E stocks are perceived as being less so.

> Logically, as the economy and corporate profits contract, the lower P/E stocks will be more impacted from an anticipated decline in earnings. As corporate profits expand, the lower P/E stocks are pulled along by rising profits and by occasional P/E expansions.

> An obvious inference to draw is that since the relative P/E of the low group fluctuates within a much narrower band than that of the high P/E group, the superior absolute returns of the former are largely due to the coincident expansion of earnings in the recovery phase of the economic expansion. Hence the greater reaction of low P/E stocks to actual or anticipated changes in economic activity (p. 23).

What do we do with this information? Capaldi says:

> The investment implications that can be drawn from this brief

analysis are fairly straightforward. The probability of achieving superior returns by investing in low P/E stocks is extremely high in any given year, except during the early stages of an economic slowdown. The "optimal" time to position portfolios to benefit from the "low P/E phenomenon" is during the depths of an economic recession when earnings are declining and pessimism is rampant (p. 23).

Capaldi's contribution was in updating the long-term low P/E-ratio study and in pointing out that even greater above-average returns can be achieved if the investor can successfully determine where he is in the economic cycle — beginning, middle, or end. As the reader knows, we believe that forecasting the level of economic activity cannot be done accurately enough or consistently enough to be useful in deciding when or when not to invest funds.

A later chapter discusses a method to use in looking at an individual company's fundamentals and at its stock price in a way that will reveal whether that issue is undervalued or overvalued. By using this approach, one can achieve the same effect that Capaldi is trying to achieve, but with a set of facts that do not rely on forecasting.

John W. Peavy, III, and David A. Goodman. John W. Peavy, III, is assistant professor of finance, and David A. Goodman is associate professor of management science and computers at the Edwin L. Cox School of Business, Southern Methodist University, Dallas.

Peavy and Goodman set out to determine whether an investor can achieve above-average rates of return, adjusted for risk by acquiring a portfolio of low P/E-ratio stocks. In their study, they wanted to eliminate any factor not related to P/E ratio that might lead to abnormal returns.[14] The three non-P/E-ratio related factors were,

1. The small-firm effect.
2. The infrequent trading effect.
3. The industry effect.

The point of the study was to obtain a clear view of whether low P/E-ratio selection and *low P/E-ratio selection only* was responsible for the above-average rates of return.

Peavy and Goodman eliminated the "small-firm effect" by eliminating any company with a market value less than $100 million. The "infrequent-trading effect" actually resulted in companies not actively traded having a reported risk factor, beta, lower than their true risk, or beta. This caused infrequently traded stocks to show above-average or abnormal rates of return in relation to their reported beta, or risk factor. To eliminate the "infrequent-trading effect," Peavy and Goodman eliminated stocks that did not have an average monthly trading volume of 25,000 shares, and no stock's trading volume was less than 10,000 shares in any month. In addition, risk calculations were done over three-month periods to eliminate the "intervaling problem," that is, the calculation of risk by using small trading intervals, such as daily, which artificially lowered the beta reading.

The "industry effect" is caused by some industries, such as the food industry, having low P/Es, and other industries, such as the electronics industry, having high P/E ratios. The problem is that, if all stocks are taken as a group and screened for low P/E ratios, all the food stocks would be included, while all the electronics stocks would be excluded. The abnormal returns experienced by low P/E-ratio stocks could then be an industry effect rather than a P/E-ratio effect.

Peavy and Goodman eliminated this problem by analyzing stocks by industry classification. The securities used were from the electronics, paper/container, and food industries. Each industry was alternatively analyzed. These industries were chosen to provide samples of stocks with higher-than-average, and lower-than-average market price volatility, beta.

The stocks used were obtained from the Compustat data tapes. Forty stocks were chosen for each industry segment. The general criteria were,

1. The fiscal year must end on December 31 or quarterly intervals—March, June, September.
2. The stock must have traded continuously from December 31, 1969, to June 30, 1980.
3. The average monthly trading volume must be 25,000 shares or more.
4. The company must have a market value in 1980 of at least $100 million.
5. All data must be available for relevant return, risk, and accounting.

There were 120 stocks in the total sample. In addition, Peavy and Goodman used the Standard & Poor's 500 Index and the 91-day Treasury Bill interest rate as substitutes for the stock market return and for the risk-free rate of return.

The stocks in each industry sample were ranked by P/E ratio and grouped into portfolio quintiles. Quarterly returns were then calculated on each of these quintiles, assuming equal initial investments in each stock. The composition of the portfolio was adjusted quarterly to reflect changing P/E ratios.

The results of Peavy and Goodman's study are shown in Table 4-27.

Table 4-27. Summary of results: January 1970–July 1980.

Industry	(LOW) 1	Price to Earnings 2	3	4	(HIGH) 5	Industry Mean
Electronics						
Number of stocks . . .	8.0	8.0	8.0	8.0	8.0	40.0
Mean quarterly return	9.24	5.45	5.11	2.96	2.21	5.05
Mean quarterly return*	8.53	4.71	4.34	2.53	1.86	4.51
Mean P/E ratio	7.1	10.3	13.4	17.4	25.5	14.7
Mean beta	1.15	1.12	1.13	1.19	1.29	1.18
Paper/container						
Number of stocks . . .	8.0	8.0	8.0	8.0	8.0	40.0
Mean quarterly return	5.37	3.40	3.99	2.38	0.94	3.41
Mean quarterly return*	5.26	3.29	4.21	2.21	0.83	3.28
Mean P/E ratio	6.7	8.5	10.2	12.4	20.2	11.6
Mean beta	1.02	1.02	1.00	1.03	1.02	1.02
Food						
Number of stocks . . .	8.0	8.0	8.0	8.0	8.0	40.0
Mean quarterly return	5.53	3.79	2.70	0.81	0.65	2.83
Mean quarterly return*	5.97	4.12	2.97	0.89	0.71	3.04
Mean P/E ratio	7.2	9.5	11.1	12.8	16.8	11.5
Mean beta	0.90	0.85	0.86	0.86	0.90	0.87

* Risk-adjusted.
Source: Peavy and Goodman, "The Significance of P/Es," p. 46.

Table 4-27 reveals that the low P/E-ratio portfolios substantially outperformed the high P/E-ratio portfolios in all industries. In addition, the returns became greater as one moved down the P/E-ratio ladder from the high P/E-ratio quintile to the low P/E-ratio quintile.

Remember from chapter 1 that the premise of "modern portfolio theory" is that a particular asset will generate a higher-than-market return *only* if that asset has a higher-than-market risk, beta, or that a low P/E-ratio portfolio should outperform the market *only* if it has a higher-than-market risk, beta.

Table 4-27 shows that contrary to the "modern portfolio theory's" "capital asset pricing model," the higher returns experienced by the low P/E-ratio portfolio were not characterized by higher levels of systematic risk, higher betas, In fact, the opposite occurred in the electronics industry. The high P/E-ratio portfolio had the highest beta but had the lowest performance.

Peavy and Goodman added additional statistical tests to the data to prove the significance of the studies. The statistical results "reinforce the contention that portfolio returns vary inversely with the magnitude of the portfolios' average P/E ratio" (p. 47). In other words, the high P/E-ratio stocks underperformed the low P/E-ratio stocks.

In another study, Peavy and Goodman related the P/E-ratio effect with firm size.[15] First, Peavy and Goodman proved again the above-average return, without additional risk, of low price-to-earnings ratio stocks. They randomly picked 125 industrial common stocks from January 1, 1970, to June 30, 1980, and adjusted the portfolio quarterly. In addition, they factored risk, or beta, by noting the beta of each P/E-ratio quintile and by adjusting the returns for risk. This gives "mean excess percentage return." Table 4-28 gives the results.

Table 4-28. January 1, 1970 to May 30, 1980.

P/E Quintile	P/E Mean	Beta	Mean Excess Percentage Returns	Absolute Rate of Return
PE1 (low)	7.1	0.92	2.80	2.48
PE2	9.5	0.95	1.51	0.71
PE3	11.4	0.98	− 0.47	0.52
PE4	14.3	1.02	− 1.42	− 0.79
PE5 (high)	25.0	1.16	− 2.42	− 1.67

Source: Peavy and Goodman, "The Interaction of Firm Size," Appendix.

Over the 10-year time period, it can be seen that the low P/E-ratio has a "mean excess percentage return" of 2.8%, i.e., 2.8% higher than the average return suggested by its systematic risk level. Contrarily, the highest P/E ratio, P/E 5, has a "mean excess percentage return" − 2.42% lower than the return implied by its systematic risk level. The returns improved on a risk-adjusted basis as they moved down the P/E-ratio levels.

Second, Peavy and Goodman ran the test using firm size as an indicator of portfolio returns. They took the same 125 companies, ranked them by firm size into five groups, then adjusted for systematic risk. FS1 are the smallest firms; FS5 are the largest firms. Table 4-29 shows the results.

Table 4-29. Mean quarterly excess returns of firm size (FS) portfolios.

Quintile	Mean (Million $)	Beta	Mean Excess Percentage Returns	Absolute Rate of Return
FS1 (small)	25.5	1.14	1.30	1.14
FS2	85.3	1.04	1.04	0.59
FS3	225.8	0.98	0.12	0.02
FS4	562.5	0.99	− 0.86	− 0.58
FS5 (large)	986.4	0.91	− 1.61	− 1.17

Source: Peavy and Goodman, "The Interaction of Firm Size," Appendix.

As the table shows, in FS1, the smallest firms, the risk-adjusted performance was 1.3% better than that implied by its risk factor. Contrarily, the risk-adjusted performance by FS5, the largest firms, was 1.6% worse than that implied by its risk factor. As the firms' sizes increased, the risk-adjusted return dropped. These findings indicate that a significant size-of-firm effect exists together with the previous P/E-ratio effect.

Third, Peavy and Goodman ran tests on the interaction of P/E ratio and firm-size effects. Is one a proxy for the other, or are the results independent of one another? If they are independent, are they cumulative in their performance effects?

First, Peavy and Goodman ran studies on the "firm-size" effect within each P/E-ratio quintile. The stocks were ranked by their price-to-earnings ratios into five groups, P/E1 being the lowest, P/E5 being the highest. Within each P/E-ratio group, the companies were divided into five groups by firm size, FS1 the smallest, FS5, the largest. The results are in Table 4-30.

This study shows that segregation by P/E ratio and segregation by firm size *do not* show that firm size produces an excess return that differs significantly across the various size-quintile categories. However, there is a microsize effect that appears in the two lowest P/E-ratio quintiles. The average return for the P/E1 quintile is 2.8%, and the smallest firms within this quintile averaged 5.08%. Perhaps this is evidence that, in the low P/E-ratio groups, firm size can be a cumulative return factor.

Table 4-30. Mean quarterly excess returns by firm size (P/E controlled).

P/E Quintile	Average	FS1	FS2	FS Quintile FS3	FS4	FS5
PE1..............	2.80	5.08	3.81	2.86	−0.04	2.29
PE2..............		2.52	2.25	1.82	0.89	0.07
PE3.............		−0.93	−0.01	0.46	−0.42	−1.45
PE4.............		−0.65	−1.36	−2.26	−1.08	−1.73
PE5.............		−2.61	−2.89	−1.39	−2.63	−2.60

Source: Peavy and Goodman, "The Interaction of Firm Size," Appendix.

Second, Peavy and Goodman ran studies of the P/E-ratio effect within each "firm-size" quintile. The stocks were ranked by their "firm size" into five groups, FS1 the smallest, FS5 the largest; then, within each FS group, the companies were divided into five groups by P/E ratios, P/E1 the lowest, P/E5 the highest. These results are in Table 4-31.

Table 4-31. Mean quarterly excess returns by P/E ratio (firm-size controlled).

P/E Quintile	(Small) FS1	FS2	FS Quintile FS3	FS4	(Large) FS5
PE1 (low)	4.52	2.98	2.34	1.30	−0.96
PE2..............	2.72	2.28	0.99	−0.02	−0.37
PE3..............	2.13	1.01	1.81	−0.22	−1.64
PE4..............	0.29	−0.85	−2.40	−2.73	−2.46
PE5 (high)	−3.16	−0.21	−2.12	−2.61	−2.64

Source: Peavy and Goodman, "The Interaction of Firm Size," Appendix.

This study shows that, with segregation by "firm size" and then division of the companies by P/E ratio, the P/E-ratio effect is significant, even after accounting for the impact of firm size. The P/E-ratio effect appears across all size quintiles. These studies show that the P/E-ratio effect is much more important than the size effect. But, in the two lower quintiles of "firm size," if low P/E qualifiers are added, the returns are cumulative, therefore higher. The conclusion to be drawn from the second major study by Peavy and Goodman is that low P/E-ratio is the major determinant in generating high returns, but that small firm size, when combined with a low P/E-ratio, can make the return even higher on a risk-adjusted basis. Admittedly, there is a great deal of controversy about this cumulative effect of small firm size, but low P/E-ratio stock selection continues its proven track record in yet another study (pp. 1-10).

Conclusion

Using statistical studies done over a span of 68 years by 16 different people, chapters 2 and 4 and Appendix C show that low price-to-earnings ratio common stocks, when selected as a group with the only criteron being low price-to-earnings ratio, consistently outperform the general market averages and high P/E-ratio stocks. This historical review of the evidence should in no way be taken as being exhaustive. To achieve that, you would have to find every article we have drawn from, locate ones we probably missed, and study them first-hand. For the reader's purpose, the evidence presented should be conclusive enough to be of great practical value in investing. For those wanting even more statistical proof and the researchers' observations, Appendix C has additional studies.

References

1. Benjamin Graham, *The Intelligent Investor: A Book of Practical Counsel,* 3rd ed. (New York: Harper & Brothers, 1959).
2. Benjamin Graham, *The Intelligent Investor: A Book of Practical Counsel,* 4th ed. (New York: Harper & Row, 1973).
3. Charles D. Ellis, "A Conversation with Benjamin Graham," *Financial Analysts Journal,* September-October 1976, p. 23.
4. S. Francis Nicholson, "Price-Earnings Ratios," *The Financial Analysts Journal,* July-August 1960, p. 43.
5. Nicholas Molodovsky, "Recent Studies of P/E Ratios," *Financial Analysts Journal,* May-June 1967, p. 101.
6. S. Francis Nicholson, "Price Ratios in Relation to Investment Results," *Financial Analysts Journal,* January-February 1968, p. 105.
7. Paul F. Miller, "Drexel & Co. Monthly Review," *Drexel & Co.,* October 1966.
8. Paul F. Miller and Ernest R. Widmann, "Price Performance Outlook For High & Low P/E Stocks," 1966 Stock and Bond Issue, *The Commercial and Financial Chronicle,* September 29, 1966.
9. Benjamin Graham, *The Intelligent Investor: A Book of Practical Counsel,* 4th ed. (New York: Harper & Row, 1973), p. 80.
10. David Dreman, *Contrarian Investment Strategy: The Psychology of Stock Market Success,* (New York: Random House, 1979), p. 131.
11. W. Anthony Hitschler, "To Know What We Don't Know or the Caribou Weren't In the Estimates," *Financial Analysts Journal,* January-February 1980, pp. 28-32.
12. W. Anthony Hitschler, "Study Results From December 1958 through December 1978 Using Total Sample," *Provident Capital Management, Inc.,* Private unpublished study. Used by permission.
13. Benedict E. Capaldi, Jr., "Low P/Es: Optimal investing: The Stage is currently being set for a recovery of these Stocks," *Pension & Investment Age,* December 6, 1982, p. 23.
14. John W. Peavy III and David A. Goodman, "The Significance of P/Es for Portfolio Returns," *The Journal of Portfolio Management,* Winter 1983.
15. John W. Peavy, III, and David A. Goodman, "The Interaction of Firm Size and Price-Earnings Ratios on Portfolio Performance," *Edwin L. Cox School of Business, Southern Methodist University,* Dallas, March 1983, Appendix.

CHAPTER 5

Comparing Investment Alternatives

Over the past two years, common stocks have performed rather well and the stock market has received much media exposure. This has not always been the case, and we recognize that some readers may question our emphasis on common stocks.

This chapter presents an abbreviated historical view of investment alternatives, including tangibles and intangibles for two different time periods. The tangibles include the popular inflation hedges of gold, silver, diamonds, and real estate (represented by raw farmland), while the financial assets include treasury bills, treasury bonds, and common stocks.

Two time periods have been chosen for the comparison, the most recent 15-year period and the most recent 56-year period. In our opinion, the longer time period is more representative of the returns that can be expected and the relative returns among the various assets. Short-term periods can be distorted by nonrecurring political and economic forces. More will be said about these forces as the comparisons are presented.

The short-term study

Periodically, Salomon Brothers, a major Wall Street brokerage firm, prepares a report that gives the compound performance figures for many popular investment instruments.[1]

Table 5-1 presents several of the assets we are focusing on and their performance for the years 1968 through mid-1983. Bear in mind that this time period was one of abnormally high inflation: The consumer price index (C.P.I.) rose 7.3% over this 15-year period, which is almost three times higher than the long-term historical rate. This is one reason tangible assets have such impressive recent results compared to the financial assets.

Table 5-1. Compound annual rates of return.

Tangibles	15 Years	10 Years	5 Years
Gold	16.6%	15.5%	17.5%
Silver	12.6%	17.3%	19.7%
Diamonds	10.1%	10.3%	5.4%
Farmland	10.0%	11.7%	7.0%
Financial			
Treasury bills	8.8%	10.1%	12.8%
Long-term gov't bonds	6.4%	6.6%	7.2%
Common stocks	5.7%	7.5%	14.8%
CPI	7.3%	8.5%	9.1%

Source: R. S. Salomon, Jr., "Financial Assets—Return to Favor," *Salomon Brothers Inc. Investment Policy,* June 10, 1983, pp. 1-4.

Investors often are overly influenced by recent performance figures. We have observed that most investors are sold their investments rather than analyzing the assets themselves and buying what they believe are the most undervalued.

Sales presentations often utilize recent performance statistics with the idea that the future will be similar to the past. Selling what is in vogue is easier than selling what is out of favor.

These recent figures would indicate that tangible assets are excellent inflation hedges, and, if the investor thinks high inflation will be a problem in the future, he should emphasize such holdings. As we mentioned earlier, unusual political and economic events can influence these returns, distorting what would be a more normal return.

Between 1934 and 1971, the government fixed the price of gold at $35 an ounce. In 1971, it was raised to $42 an ounce and remained fixed until January 1, 1975. During this time period, while the official price was fixed at $42 an ounce, gold was trading in the free market at $200 an ounce as people speculated on what the price would be when U.S. citizens were allowed to own it. Since that time, gold has demonstrated considerable price volatility and varying degrees of popularity with investors.

We're not trying to present a historical analysis of gold as an investment. Rather, we believe the recent price performance is not only a result of gold being an inflation hedge, but also a result of a "catch-up" effect after the price fixing was removed. This effect has also had a similar influence on the performance of silver.

To eliminate the "catch-up" effect in precious metals, we decided to include diamonds and farmland in the tangibles category. These two assets seem to reflect inflation concerns without the extraordinary forces that affected gold.

Farmland is representative of unimproved U.S. real estate whose price is set by a free market system with knowledgeable buyers and sellers interacting. Farmland also removes the financing leverage and favorable tax treatment both commercial and residential real estate have benefited from.

While diamonds did not have a "catch-up" effect in their performance, diamond prices are not entirely set by a free market structure. DeBeers, the world's largest diamond dealer, sells about 80% of the world's supply of diamonds. As a result, the price is set by a monopoly seller, not by free market forces. You should also realize that the spread between dealer bid-and-ask prices for diamonds can be 30 to 40 percent, which will have a significant effect on investment results when the asset is sold. A dealer spread or markup is not much of a consideration in precious metals, farmland, or financial assets.

The investor in tangible assets did rather well during the period between 1968 and 1983. However, while tangibles were benefiting from the unusual circumstances, financial assets were being penalized by other unusual occurrences. By taking these factors into account, you will be better able to understand the performance figures given in Table 5-1.

From the late 1940s through the 1960s, common stocks experienced a long bull market with only periodic setbacks. This advance was fueled by the post-World War II economic expansion and the increasing acceptance of common stocks. By the late 1960s stocks had advanced to a level that was no longer realistic in relation to the underlying values of the corporations they represented. There was much speculation near the end, as gains fueled additional purchases.

In late 1968, the starting point of the 15-year study shown in Table 5-1, a market correction began that lasted until late 1974. This is considered to be one of the more severe bear markets in history. The market retreated from a level of high overvaluation to one of extreme undervaluation in a period of eight years. This downward bias in share prices can best be shown in one of David Dreman's studies focusing on the August 1968 to August 1977 time period.[2]

Table 5-2. Annualized compound rates of return, August 1968-August 1977 (full period of study).

Stocks Ranked by P/E Multiples Decile	1 Quarter	Switching After Each: 6 Months	1 Year	3 Years	Holding Original Portfolio for 9 Years
1 (highest)	− 2.64%	− 1.06%	− 1.13%	− 1.43%	0.33%
2	0.92	1.62	0.56	− 0.28	1.27
3	0.51	0.62	1.63	0.85	3.30
4	3.06	3.42	3.31	4.87	5.36
5	2.19	4.46	2.93	5.02	3.72
6	4.84	5.33	6.70	4.82	4.52
7	7.90	6.07	6.85	5.89	6.08
8	8.83	8.24	8.56	7.78	6.35
9	11.85	8.40	6.08	7.73	6.40
10 (lowest)	14.00	11.68	10.26	10.89	7.89

Average return of sample............4.75%

Source: David Dreman, *Contrarian Investment Strategy*, p. 131.

Two points are worth noting. First, during this time period, low P/E-ratio stocks still outperformed high P/E-ratio stocks and had respectable positive rates of return. Second, the average return for the sample is 4.75%, roughly one half of the long-term results for common stocks. This study ends in 1977, and at that time stocks were still considered cheap on a valuation basis. You should bear in mind that these below-average returns have biased downward the 10- and 15-year results in Table 5-1 for common stocks.

Another financial asset that did rather poorly during the 1970s, especially during the late 1970s and early 1980s, is bonds. Chart 5-1 shows the historical trend in interest rates going back to 1929.[3]

Chart 5-1. Industrial bond yields by ratings (long-term monthly averages).

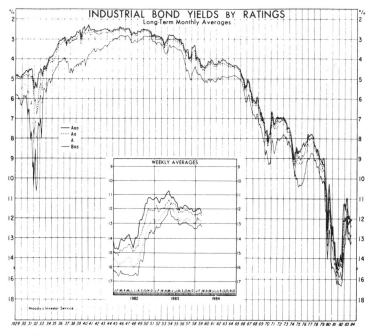

Source: "Moody's Bond Record," p. 239.

Since World War II, interest rates have been in a secular rise, and this rise accelerated in the late 1970s. To combat the high levels of inflation, the Federal Reserve Bank embarked on a policy that was more monetarist than had previously existed. Before this, the Federal Reserve focused on keeping interest rates at acceptable levels and paid little attention to the expansion of the monetary aggregates. Their focus shifted in the late 1970s, and, as the "Fed" reduced money growth, interest rates rose to unprecedented highs. The bonds that were already outstanding declined in price to be competitive with the new, higher coupons that the market required. Holders of long-maturity bonds experienced negative returns during this policy shift, and these returns had an impact on the performance figures, as shown in Table 5-1.

Should an investor rely on this short-term study to allocate his investable funds? Were there unusual events in the past five to fifteen years that will probably not occur again? As we said, we don't believe anyone can forecast the future. We do believe the long-term study gives a better picture of the relationship between tangible and intangible assets.

The long-term study

In *Stocks, Bonds, Bills and Inflation: The Past and the Future,* Roger G. Ibbotson and Rex A. Sinquefield give the long-term rates of return for financial assets. Table 5-3 lists the 56-year compound rates of return Ibbotson and Sinquefield calculated for financial assets such as treasury bills, long-term-government bonds, and common stocks.[4] From several sources we calculated the rates of return for gold, silver, diamonds, and farmland. We also added the rate of return for low P/E-ratio common stocks, which we derived from linking together several studies (included in this book) and by double-checking our result against Ben Graham's long-term results.

Table 5-3. Compound annual rates of return (1926-1981).

Tangibles	56 Years
Gold	5.7%
Silver	5.5%
Diamonds	4.8%
Farmland	4.6%
Financial	
Treasury Bills.	3.0%
L.T. govt. bonds	3.0%
Common stocks	9.1%
Low P/E-ratio stocks	15.0%
CPI	3.0%

Sources: Tangibles—Asset prices computed from other sources.

Financial—Ibbotson and Sinquefield, p. 4.

Low P/E-ratio common stock performance derived from the low P/E studies described in chapters 2 and 4 and Appendix C.

The long-term results (Table 5-3) indicate that treasury bills and bonds will return the inflation rate on a pretax basis. If taxes are taken into account, the investor would experience a negative return in fixed-income instruments. However, fixed-income instruments are the starting point of any proper investment program: They provide a value benchmark against which other investments can be measured.

The key incentive in selecting common stocks is to improve on the return that can be earned by passive, fixed-income instruments. If that return cannot be improved on, the investor is not compensated for the increased risk he has assumed by owning common stocks.

Also, by using prevailing bond yields as valuation benchmarks, the investor can avoid being invested in stocks when they are extremely over-valued, as in the late 1960s. By being in intermediate bonds at that time, the investor would have preserved capital. He would have been ready to make commitments in the bear market of the early 1970s. Bonds, although not necessarily a good long-term investment, do have their role in the investment process.

We believe that tangible assets over a long time period will provide a return that will exceed inflation. According to the long-term study on the various investment alternatives, gold had a return of 5.7%, while the consumer price index rose 3%. This return above the inflation rate is the result of supply-and-demand forces unique to that particular asset. For gold (and silver) this additional return may be attributable to industrial influences or political considerations. For farmland, the return may reflect inflation plus anticipated returns due to economic improvements and alternative economic uses. Tangible assets can be useful in *preserving* wealth. They do not, however, provide a high enough excess return to *build* wealth.

The highest return in the long-term study (see Table 5-3) was recorded by common stocks at 9.1%, well over inflation and all the other assets in both categories. We have included in this table a long-term-return figure for low P/E-ratio stocks of 15%. As mentioned earlier, this is a number derived from all the studies presented in chapters 2, 4, Appendix C.

Although we make no predictions about the future, we believe these relationships (in Table 5-3) should continue with some consistency. For example, we think common stocks will provide a superior return over a long period as given in chapter 3's discussion on how corporations build wealth for their owners. Unlike fixed-income instruments and tangible assets, common stocks represent an ownership interest in growing productive enterprises. If chosen correctly, common stocks will not merely protect wealth, but can actually build wealth. The investor must recognize, however, that, with current inflation rates at higher levels than previously experienced, the stock selection process becomes more critical. No longer can you profitably own shares in just any industrial corporation. An investor must select companies that can generate real profits after inflation and can sustain above-average rates of return on invested capital. It is these characteristics that will enable the investor to compound his wealth and prosper in any economic environment.

References

1. R. S. Salomon, Jr., "Financial Assets—Return to Favor," *Salomon Brothers Inc. Investment Policy,* June 10, 1983.
2. David Dreman, *Contrarian Investment Strategy: The Psychology of Stock Market Success* (New York: Random House, 1979).
3. "Moody's Bond Record" Vol. 51, No. 3, *Moody's Investors Service, Inc.,* New York, March 1984.
4. Roger G. Ibbotson and Rex A. Sinquefield, *Stocks, Bonds, Bills and Inflation: The Past and The Future,* 1982 ed., The Financial Analysts Research Foundation, University of Virginia, Charlottesville, Virginia, 1982.

CHAPTER 6

How to Make Compound Interest Work for You

Greed and unrealistic expectations!—two personality traits that lead to investment losses. As we said earlier, most investors get caught up in the *price effect* of investing. For them, one profits from investments by buying a stock at $20 and selling it at $30, making a 50% gain. We have also observed that, as bull markets mature, investors' time horizons often shorten. Expectations of returns increase as a result of the large gains made in the early stages of the advance. Instead of becoming cautious, the investor begins to anticipate 50% gains in less than a year.

Our approach to investing focuses on the financial dynamics of a corporation and how an investor can compound his wealth as the company grows. We suggest letting others try for the 50% to 100% returns in one year or less. We submit that the true investor seeks out companies that will enable him to compound at 14%, the estimated long-term return on equity capital.

While that number may appear at first to be a low expectation, consider an example: Suppose an investor, when he begins his working career, bought $5,000 worth of stock in a company at book value. Suppose the company compounds its book value over the next forty years at 14%. At retirement, if the investor sold his stock at book value, his $5,000 would be worth $944,417.57. In other words, in one's typical career span, a person can become worth almost one million dollars. Our idea is to let everyone else try the get-rich-quick schemes, while we use compound interest to get rich slowly, but with much greater certainty.

The investor who wants to accumulate wealth through compound interest has available many financial asset choices. Four of the most common are described here. Take a moment to note their similarities and their differences.

If *money market funds* are selected on the basis of quality, there is very little risk to the principal investment. The investor enjoys instant availability of his funds. The rate earned on principal, however, can fluctuate widely. The income is received in cash, which is added to the fund. But, since the interest rate is quite volatile, it is difficult to determine the rate at which the principal will compound.

Certificates of deposit are backed by the Federal Deposit Insurance Corporation up to $100,000 and involve very little risk. Generally, principal is committed to a certificate of deposit for a specified period of time — 3 months, 6 months, 18 months, or longer. The income is received in cash, and the interest rate is guaranteed until the certificate matures. At that time the certificate can be renewed at the original rate or at a higher rate, or a lower rate. Variability of the rate at reinvestment is what is known as the "reinvestment risk."

Bonds vary in quality from no-risk U.S. Government bonds to low-quality corporate bonds, those that are rated to be near default. The principal is only as safe as the entity in which it is invested. The principal will be redeemed in full at maturity, which in some cases can be as long as 40 years. The coupon rate is fixed for the life of the bond.

Between the time the bond is acquired and the time at which it matures, the principal value can fluctuate in the market, depending on the interest rates available on other instruments and on perceived changes in the bond's quality. The income is received in cash. The bond buyer also faces the "reinvestment risk" on the reinvestment of the income stream, as it is received, and on the principal at maturity.

With *common stock investments,* safety of principal is not guaranteed. The common stock investor is the last to be satisfied, behind the creditors, in the event of liquidation of the company. The common stock investor receives part of his income in cash dividends. Part remains to be reinvested at whatever rate the corporation can earn on its invested capital. Some companies consistently earn a competitively high return on their invested capital. Equity investments in these companies reduce, for the most part, the "reinvestment risk" for long-term compounding. (We'll say more about these types of companies in the next two chapters.)

The principal value also will fluctuate with equity investments. However, the investor usually enjoys quick availability of his invested funds particularly if the investment is in a company whose stock is widely held.

This list of options for investment in financial assets is certainly not exhaustive. Over the past several years, with double-digit inflation and high interest rates, several hybrid securities have been introduced, such as floating-rate notes and zero-coupon bonds. While it is beyond the scope of this work to describe all the alternatives and their advantages and disadvantages, our brief list contains the items most familiar to the reader and points out positives and negatives of each investment.

In our opinion, the important characteristics on which to focus for any financial asset are (1) safety of principal, or of the enterprise in which it is invested; (2) how the income is received, in cash or by reinvestment; and (3) the "reinvestment risk" of income and principal. By understanding these concepts, the investor can compare stocks to other alternatives and determine the values of each.

In our opinion, investment should be thought of as a process of wealth accumulation through compound interest. This can easily be demonstrated and explained by the following example.

Assume an investor acquires a $1,000 bond that pays $120 per year, i.e., a 12% coupon rate, and matures in six years. Also assume that the income, $120 per year, can be reinvested at a 12% rate. The assumption made in using the term "yield-to-maturity" is that the income received can be reinvested at the same rate at which it was originally acquired. Any variance in the reinvestment rate will change the investor's realized compound "yield-to-maturity."[1]

$1,000   Original principal

720   Interest received from the coupons, $120 × 6 or $60 × 12, if semi-annual.

280   Interest received from the reinvestment of the interest earned at 12%. This is also known as the "interest on interest."

$2,000   Total principal, interest, and reinvestment income. For money to double at 12%, it takes 6.11 years. For purposes of illustration, we used six years.

With bond investments, the principal is paid at maturity, the income is received in cash, and the major risk is the "reinvestment risk." This can be calculated for any fixed-income investment. But how can these be compared with common stock investments?

The investor's equation

With the aid of a standard business calculator or a compound interest table, the investor can easily compare investment alternatives. Here is a procedure to express the value of a stock on the same basis as a bond's yield-to-maturity.[2]

Assume that a company's stock sells at book value and can consistently earn a 14% return on its equity capital. This results in earnings of $7 on a $50 stock—$50 times 14%. Next, assume that the company pays 40% of its earnings in dividends, which will be used by the investor to purchase more stock in the open market. As in figuring yield-to-maturity where reinvestment rates are assumed, we assume that the stock will always sell at book value. The other 60% of earnings is retained by the company to acquire more assets that can earn 14% on invested capital.

Table 6-1.

Market price	$50
Earnings per share	$ 7
P/E ratio	7.14 ×
Earnings yield: 1 divided by 7.14	14%
Book value	$50
Return on equity: 7 divided by 50	14%
Dividend	$ 2.80
Dividend yield	5.6%
Reinvestment rate: % of earnings retained multiplied by the return on equity, .60 × 14	8.4%
Total return: reinvestment rate plus the dividend yield	14%

For every dollar invested, the investor receives an earnings annuity of $.14 that will grow at 14%. The earnings annuity is the reciprocal of the price-earnings ratio, also called the "earnings yield." The growth rate is an arithmetic weighting of the dividend yield and the internal reinvestment rate. The yield is the dividend divided by the market price; the internal reinvestment rate is the percentage of the earnings that are retained, multiplied by the return-on-equity. The total return is 14%, a 5.6% dividend yield plus an 8.4% reinvestment rate. By using a business calculator with a compound interest function, we find that $7 in earnings compounding at 14% will equal $50, our original investment, in 5.29 years. In other words, if the stock sells at book value, the investor will double his investment in 5.29 years.

What happens when the same company's stock sells at a price above book value?

Table 6-2.

Market price	$60
Earnings per share	$ 7
P/E ratio	8.57×
Earnings yield: 1 divided by 8.57	11.66%
Book value	$50
Return on equity: 7 divided by 50	14%
Dividend	$ 2.80
Dividend yield	4.6%
Reinvestment rate: % of earnings retained multiplied by the return on equity, .60 × 14	8.4%
Total return; reinvestment rate plus the dividend yield	13%

In this case, the investor pays 120% of book value, $60, and receives a dividend yield of 4.6%. The earnings yield is 11.66% on the same earnings as in Table 6-1, but a higher price was paid. The higher price reduces the return received. The internal reinvestment rate remains the same at 8.4% ($60 × 14% return on equity), since the reinvested earnings are invested at book value.

We assume the stock will continue to sell at 120% of book value. Therefore, the earnings yield of 11.66% will compound at a total return rate of 13%. If the stock sells at 120% of book value, the investor doubles his investment in 6.13 years.

This is the equivalent of buying a bond with an 11.97% yield-to-maturity, as contrasted to the first example, which had an equivalent of a 14% yield-to-maturity.

What caused the difference in returns? Well, when a stock is purchased at book value, its price-to-earnings ratio is the reciprocal of the return on equity, and its earnings yield is the same as the return on equity. When an investor purchases a stock above book value, however, the P/E ratio is increased and the dividend yield is reduced. The earnings yield declines from 14% to 11.66%, and the total return—reinvestment rate plus yield (which becomes the compounding rate)—declines from 14% to 13%. In other words, the investor received less in earnings, which were compounded at a lower rate, resulting in less long-term wealth.

What happens when a stock with the same return on equity and dividend payout is purchased *below* book value?

Table 6-3.

Market price	$40
Earnings per share	$ 7
P/E ratio	5.7 ×
Earnings yield: 1 divided by 5.7	17.5%
Book value	$50
Return on equity: 7 divided by 50	14%
Dividend	$ 2.80
Dividend yield	7%
Reinvestment rate: % of earnings retained multiplied by the return on equity, .60 × 14	8.4%
Total return; reinvestment rate plus the dividend yield	15.4%

The investor receives an earnings yield of 17.5% that will compound at 15.4%. He will double his investment in 4.40 years. This is the equivalent of a bond having a 17.06% yield-to-maturity. Because the stock was purchased, in this example, below book value, more earnings were received as well as a higher compounding rate. It is logical that the investor receives more for his invested dollar when he purchases a stock priced below book value.

These examples help to demonstrate several relationships in figuring the value received from an investment:

First, the lower the price-earnings ratio, the closer to book value or below book value the stock will sell.

Second, the lower the price-earnings ratio, the higher the earnings yield.

Third, assuming no taxes, the investor benefits more by purchasing a stock priced below its book value, receiving dividends, and then reinvesting those dividends at a price below book value than he would by having the corporation retain those dividends and reinvesting them at book value.

Fourth, if a stock sells above book value, the investor benefits more when the company pays less in dividends, since the earnings retained are reinvested at book value, rather than purchasing additional shares above book value.

Five, the ratios of dividend payout, earnings retention, and normal return on equity are all very important points to consider in determining the weighted-average-return for compounding purposes.

The authors recognize that the book value of the stock of a corporation does not represent the replacement value of the assets of the corporation. Book value is an accounting concept, like earnings, the return received from the owner's assets. We believe that book value is to the stock investor what the par or principal amount is to a bond investor with the sustainable return-on-equity being the same as the coupon or interest rate on a bond.

As shown in the examples, the stock with a return-on-equity of 14%, which is selling at book value, has a quicker payback than a bond with a 12% coupon rate selling at par value.

In its simplest form, the "investor's equation" takes the earnings yield—the reciprocal of the P/E ratio—and compounds this yield at the stock's total-return figure. That figure is the internal reinvestment rate plus the dividend yield at the time of purchase. The length of time it takes for this yield to equal one is called the "payback" period, or the time in which the stock will double in value, assuming it sells at the same price-to-book value relationship.

Using a business calculator or a compound interest table, you can figure a bond yield-to-maturity equivalent for a stock by calculating the interest rate at which an investor would double his money with a bond investment for the same period of time. Let's assume a stock has a book value of $50, earns 18% return-on-equity, retains 80% of earnings, and sells at seven times earnings. The calculations would be as follows.

Table 6-4.

Market price	$63
Earnings per share	$ 9
P/E ratio	7×
Earnings yield: 1 divided by 7	14.28%
Book value	$50
Return on equity: 9 divided by 50	18%
Dividend	$ 1.80
Dividend yield	2.8%
Reinvestment rate: % of earnings retained multiplied by the return on equity, .80 × 18	14.4%
Total return; reinvestment rate plus the dividend yield	17.2%

The earnings yield of 14.28% will compound at a rate of 17.2%. If the price-to-book value remains constant and the dividends are invested in more stock, the investor will double his money in 4.98 years. This is the same time it takes for a 14.93% coupon bond to double an investor's wealth, assuming the coupon income can be reinvested at 14.93%. The reason this stock can sell above book value and still provide such a high return is its high return-on-equity and its low dividend payout. Eighty percent of the earnings are being reinvested at book value to earn a high rate of 18%. Notice, however, that the P/E ratio is still a low seven-times-earnings, again demonstrating the value of low P/E-ratio stocks.

The "investor's equation,"—the earnings yield compounding at the total return rate—can be used to compare stocks to bonds and stocks to stocks. The investor needs to keep in mind that bonds will eventually mature, and that the coupon income is received in cash. The investor faces a "reinvestment risk" with the cash flows and with the proceeds at maturity.

The stock investor, on the other hand, owns a perpetual investment with earnings paid partly in cash and partly reinvested at book value. The stock investor, in other words, does not face the reinvestment risk faced by the bond investor, *if* he invests in companies that maintain a competitive return-on-invested-capital.

In the next chapter, we present several variations of the low P/E-ratio philosophy. As you consider these variations, you should bear in mind three more obstacles to obtaining a satisfactory return on your investment. These obstacles are brokerage commissions, taxes, and inflation.

The first obstacle is being reduced, in part, by the entrance of numerous firms into the discount brokerage business. One has to wonder if Wall Street is not currently going to another extreme with the result that, when the next bear market arrives, more firms will be willing to discount than there are customers willing to invest. In the meantime, the individual can surmount at least one of the three obstacles by negotiation. The other two are not as easy.

Over the past two years, marginal taxes have been reduced. The economy currently is enjoying a cyclical respite from inflation. Although political and economic trends are beyond the scope of this work (and we do not believe in forecasting), the investor should be alert to the re-emergence of both higher taxes and higher inflation. In any event, the prospective investor should weigh tax-free bonds against the attractiveness of stocks and should, when possible, postpone realizing profits and incurring a tax liability. The examples of calculating rates of return can easily be adjusted for the effects of taxes and inflation. The investor simply reduces the earnings yield by the appropriate amount to allow for capital gains taxes on growth and for income taxes on dividends.

Let's take an example. Assume that a stock has a book value of $50, earns an 18% return-on-equity, retains 80% of earnings, and sells at seven times earnings and that the investor is in a marginal tax bracket of 40%. What will be the compound rate-of-return, assuming that the stock continues to sell at seven times earnings?

Table 6-5. Example: Pretax return on stock.

Market price	$63
Earnings per share	$ 9
P/E ratio	7×
Earnings yield: 1 divided by 7	14.28%
Book value	$50
Return on equity: 9 divided by 50	18%
Dividend	$ 1.80
Dividend yield	2.8%
Reinvestment rate: % of earnings retained multiplied by the return on equity, .80 × 18	14.4%
Total return; reinvestment rate plus the dividend yield	17.2%

The earnings yield of 14.28% can be divided into an annuity consisting of two parts: that portion to be paid out as a dividend and taxed as ordinary income to the investor and that portion retained by the business, reinvested at book value to grow at the sustainable return on equity and eventually taxed as a long-term capital gain.

In addition, assume the following: The investor has a marginal tax rate of 40%, and 60% of long-term capital gains are excluded from taxation, with the tax on the balance not to exceed 50%.

The following calculations give the after-tax return on the stock example above that the investor should compare against tax-free investment alternatives.

Table 6-6. Example: After-tax return on stock.

A. Dividend:

Earnings annuity 1/7	=	14.28
The dividend payout	=	× .20
		2.86

Less the taxes on the dividend at 40% (1 − .40)	=	× .60
		1.71

Because the dividend will be used to purchase more stock, the after-tax-return needs to be reduced again to allow for the taxes incurred on the stock it purchases. This factor is a weighted average of the 40% marginal rate on 20% of the investment and the long-term capital gain rate (1 − .21)

20% × 40% = 8%
80% × 16% = 12.8%
Weighted avg. tax   20.8%
    after-tax return: 1−20.8 = 79.2%

	=	× .79
After-tax return on dividend portion		1.35 1.35

B. Retained earnings:

Earnings Annuity 1/7	=	14.28
Retained earnings	=	× .80

Portion that will eventually be taxed as a long-term gain (40% will be taxed)   11.42
60% is excluded
Tax on the 40% is 40% or

16% (1 − .16)	=	× .84
After-tax return on retained-earnings portion		9.59 9.60

10.95 Total after-tax return
earnings yield on stock

You may not choose to go through this breakdown on each stock contemplated. The model, however, does show the penalty incurred on dividends. If your goal as an investor is to accumulate wealth through compounding and the reinvestment of dividends, you're much better off selecting companies that have a high return on equity and that are prepared to reinvest most if not all of a company's earnings at that above-average rate. Money paid as dividends is taxed once as normal income and then again as capital gains and dividends. Earnings retained add to the value of the company and will only be taxed once as capital gains.

The after-tax weighted earnings yield of 10.96%, converted to an annuity of 10.96¢, will grow to $1.00 at a 17.2% growth rate, total return, in 5.95 years compared to 4.98 years in the pre-tax example. The yield-to-maturity effect from an after-tax 14.93% coupon bond equivalent for the earlier example would be reduced to an after-tax 12.36% coupon bond equivalent, demonstating the tax disadvantage in investment.

In this example, note the stock's low pay-out, 20%, and its high reinvestment rate. Had the payout been closer to the norm for industrial companies, 40%, and the return-on-equity closer to average, 14%, the return would have been lower. This occurs because more of the earnings would have been paid at the higher income tax rate on dividends as against the capital gain rate on appreciated value; the retained earnings would have grown at a lower compound rate. To adjust for inflation, you should subtract the inflation rate from the coupon equivalent rate to arrive at the after-tax, after-inflation return on investment.

Coupon equivalent return 12.36%
Core inflation . . . . 7.0 %
Real after-inflation return 5.36%

Core inflation is the underlying inflation rate around which the more volatile consumer price index fluctuates. There is no official core rate; the 7% rate is an arbitrary judgment used by several economists.

For the investor in a high marginal tax bracket, it becomes critical to consider such things as dividend payouts, the sustainable return-on-equity, and, obviously, the earnings yield or P/E ratio. As changes occur in these components, high-quality tax-exempt bonds will often become more attractive than equities. By using the "investor's equation," the investor can determine the relative attractiveness of stocks and bonds.

References

1. *Inside the Yield Book: New Tools for Bond Market Strategy* (Englewood Cliffs, NJ: Prentice-Hall, 1972; New York Institute of Finance, 1972), p. 21.
2. *The Investor's Equation,* ©Bowen & Ganucheau 1984, was derived from ideas presented in Ben Graham, *The Intelligent Investor,* and Warren Buffett, "How Inflation Swindles the Equity Investors."

CHAPTER 7

Refining the Low P/E-Ratio Approach

"The habit of relating what is paid to what is being offered
is an invaluable trait in investments."
Ben Graham

Among the several definitions of "philosophy" offered by the Random House *Dictionary of The English Language* are:

1. The rational investigation of the truths and principles of being, knowledge of conduct:
2. The critical study of the basic principles and concepts of a particular branch of knowledge, especially with a view to improving or constructing them.

Understanding, adopting, and adhering to a proven investment philosophy are extremely important parts of a successful investment program. For, as Descartes summarized in *Discours de la Method* more than three centuries ago, "It is not enough to have a good intelligence, the principal thing is to apply it well." The authors would add that a good intelligence and adequate information are both necessary.

To arrive at the investment philosophy presented in this chapter, several observations and discoveries have been made and several conclusions drawn. The reader may recall that there are four basic investment philosophies in use by contemporary money managers. In summary these are:

1. The "top-down approach" focuses on forecasts of the economy and how they will have an impact on the price of various securities.
2. The "bottom-up approach" concentrates on individual stocks and uses perceived value based on forecasts of earnings for selection of the most attractive holdings.
3. "Technical analysis" uses charts and other timing devices to forecast market moves and stock movements. "Relative strength" is related to "technical analysis" and focuses on those equities currently performing the best in the belief that they will continue to do so.
4. The "modern portfolio theory" is based on the idea that the market is efficient and that there is a definite relationship between risk and return. The risk of a stock is measured by its volatility in relation to a market index, such as the Standard & Poor's 500, as well as by individual characteristics. The objective is to keep the risk, a stock's beta, low in relation to the market, and, to keep the potential, or alpha, of the individual stock high. By doing this, it is believed the investor will incur risk that is in line with the market, a beta of 1, but which will probably outperform the market because of the stock's alpha.

An investor may occasionally encounter a philosophy different from the ones mentioned above. For example, a portfolio manager may select stocks to participate in a disinflationary environment or in emerging technologies. We refer to this as "theme investing" and consider it to be a derivitive of either the "top-down" or "bottom-up" approaches.

Most philosophies in use by money managers today are forms of the four mentioned above and have the same flaws. They rely on perceptions or forecasts, either of the economy or of earnings, and focus on the movement in the price of the stock more than on the underlying realities of the corporation.

Frequently, a portfolio manager will hear a story about a stock that ends like this, "We feel the company can earn $5 this year and, with a 10 multiple, it is easily worth $50 per share."

Often two characteristics—earnings and the price-earnings ratio—are forecast to justify some target price. As discussed in chapters 1 and 3, economic forecasts are unreliable, and price-earnings ratios are more volatile than earnings. To be successful, one needs an investment philosophy that does not rely on forecasting and that can determine the real worth of a company in relation to the price of its stock. With the ability to become an owner of a share in a company for less than that share's intrinsic value, an investor can have some assurance that his principal will not be lost and that he will prosper as the company prospers.

To enable an investor to buy a stock below its intrinsic value, the market needs to be somewhat inefficient, as defined by the group that uses the "modern portfolio theory." This explains why the discovery of low P/E-ratio stock selection for stock market success was another major finding. As we said in chapters 2 and 4, this method of selection has been shown in study after study to produce consistently superior investment results over a 50-year period. Its success is shown not only in academic tests, but also in successful use by practitioners. This was the only method used in testing the "efficient market hypothesis" that failed to prove that the market was at least somewhat efficient. From these findings, we derived conclusions: One, there is a method that can lead to the superior selection of stocks and, two, although the market is inefficient in the short run, it probably is efficient over the long run. It follows that a company's stock can be purchased for less than its intrinsic value.

The next step in arriving at a philosophy was to understand and explain why low P/E-ratio stocks do (and should) give above-average results. The first explanation, and the one referred to in most articles or books regarding low P/E-ratio stocks, is the psychological one. Investors' emotions of fear and greed have a tendency to push the market to extremes, so that the prices of securities do not reflect the underlying realities of the companies in which the securities represent ownership.

These extremes provide opportunities to buy and sell when the prices over-discount or under-discount the potential of the company. These opportunities exist, however, only for the investor willing to act independently of the crowd's emotions.

Again, it becomes evident that a philosophy should be a tool that will enable an investor to determine the real worth of a corporation so that he is less likely to succumb to the emotional extremes.

The goal of being able to determine investment value encouraged us to develop a financial explanation of why low P/E-ratio stocks provide superior performance. Some investors believe that the way to make money is to buy a stock at price A and sell it at price B. Hence all the focus on price action and not on the companies. We concluded that the purpose of investment is to accumulate wealth through compound interest. This is achieved by corporations when they retain a portion of their earnings—the amount left after dividends are paid—and use these earnings to acquire more assets that will earn a competitive return. As the asset base of the corporation grows and so long as the assets can earn a competitive return, the share owners' wealth grows and does so at a compound rate.

As we discussed in chapter 5, common stocks have provided the highest return of any financial asset when viewed over an extended period. The basic philosophy we advocate concentrates on making investments in low P/E-ratio stocks. The second and third variations are refinements of the basic philosophy. Each level considers more components and requires more sophistication.

Philosophy A, the basic philosophy

All the research and evidence presented supports the view that, as a group, low P/E-ratio stocks provide the highest total return for equity investments. In its simplest form, the basic philosophy advocates that the investor should own a portfolio of low P/E-ratio stocks. This can be accomplished in several ways, the easiest being to acquire a list of stocks, such as the Standard & Poor's 500, ranked by their P/E-ratios. By selecting the 100 stocks with lowest P/E ratios, the investor will acquire a well-diversified portfolio that should have an above-average dividend yield.

The number of stocks used at this level of investment should be many—100 is recommended—to minimize the impact on the portfolio of companies that may become bankrupt or have severe financial problems. Also, by using such a large number of stocks, many industries will be represented, again helping the diversification of the portfolio.

One of the additional studies included in the appendix on researchers in the field used this "shotgun" approach to investment. The database used covered about 1,400 industrial companies. The researcher required that the companies meet three criteria. The companies' stocks had to trade on the New York Stock Exchange, have fiscal years ending on December 31, and have all relevant investment returns. Of the group of 1,400, only 500 met all these requirements over a period of 14 years. The results show that, on average, the highest P/E-ratio stocks had a return of 9.6%, the middle or average group returned 11.7%, while the lowest P/E-ratio group had a return of 16.3%.[1]

In other studies using large groups of stocks, that would be representative of the "shotgun" approach, the results are similar for low P/E-ratio stocks. In Dreman's studies, the returns are shown in Table 7-1, a very difficult market environment.

Table 7-1. Annualized compound rates of return,
August 1968 to August 1977 (full period of study).

Stocks Ranked by P/E Multiples Decile*	Switching Stocks After Each:				Holding Original Portfolio for 9 Years
	1 Quarter	6 Months	1 Year	3 Years	
1 (highest)	−2.64%	−1.06%	−1.13%	−1.43%	0.33%
2	0.92	1.62	0.56	−0.28	1.27
3	0.51	0.62	1.63	0.85	3.30
4	3.06	3.42	3.31	4.87	5.36
5	2.19	4.46	2.93	5.02	3.72
6	4.84	5.33	6.70	4.82	4.52
7	7.90	6.07	6.85	5.89	6.08
8	8.83	8.24	8.56	7.78	6.35
9	11.85	8.40	6.08	7.73	6.40
10 (lowest)	14.00	11.68	10.26	10.89	7.89

Average return of sample 4.75%

* Take all stocks in study and divide them into ten groups according to the price-to-earnings multiple.

Source: David Dreman, *Contrarian Investment Strategy: The Psychology of Stock Market Success* (New York: Random House, 1979), p. 131.

In the crudest form of the "shotgun" approach, the investor can select a compilation of stocks, such as the Standard & Poor's 500 or Value Line 900 Industrial Composite, and, from it, purchase stocks in the low P/E-ratio group. As Dreman's studies indicate, the highest results are in those portfolios that are adjusted every quarter, to keep the portfolio invested in the lowest P/E-ratio stocks.

The disadvantages to this approach are obvious. First, for the investor who has a moderate sum to invest, it would be difficult if not impossible to own stocks in 100 companies. Second, even if this approach could be followed completely, the frequent trading would make the commission costs rather high, and most gains would be short-term rather than long-term. This approach, although it could be done, would be both cumbersome and costly.

Philosophy B, the rifle approach

This philosophy also focuses on low P/E-ratio stocks. It is refined, however, so that it can be applied by individuals as well as institutions who are willing to spend a little time with their investments to benefit from low P/E-ratio stocks. The goal of this philosophy is to be able to reduce the size of the portfolio to 20 or more stocks, to reduce turnover to save on commissions, and, as much as possible, to have the capital gains be long-term for favorable tax treatment.

These goals are accomplished by using standards of quality to filter the list of low P/E-ratio stocks. Any number of standards can be used, but we think they should focus on financial soundness as well as stability and growth of shareholder equity.

Examples of standards an investor may use in this approach are, (1) low debt-to-equity ratio, (2) high dividend yield, (3) strong current ratio, (4) no loss years in the past five years, (5) earnings growth of at least 7% per year over the past five years, (6) a Standard & Poor's quality rating on the companies' bonds of A or better, and (8) an above-average return-on-equity over the past five years.

By applying some of these standards, a portfolio of high-quality stocks can be acquired that should, over the long run, provide above-average returns.

Chapter 10 includes a portfolio of stocks that the authors formed as of December 31, 1981. These companies were from a list of stocks with the lowest P/E ratios in the Standard & Poor's 400. The standards used were: (1) the P/E ratio had to be in the lowest 12½%, i.e., bottom 50, of the Standard & Poor's 400; (2) the companies had to have a Standard & Poor's stock quality rating of A – or better; and (3) the stock had to provide a dividend yield of 40% or more of the current bond yield, which was 15% at the time.

In addition, two bank stocks were chosen and added to the basic list of industrial stocks. The completed portfolio had 22 companies representing 13 industries, a fairly well-diversified portfolio. For the calendar year of 1982, the total return on the portfolio was 25% versus a total return of 20.3% for the Standard & Poor's 500.

By using several other criteria in conjunction with the main criterion of low P/E ratio, the investor should be able to construct a portfolio of 20 or more stocks. We recommend this number because of several studies done on the impact of diversification on a portfolio's return.

In Richard A. Brealey's book, *An Introduction to Risk and Return From Common Stocks,* Brealey concludes that it can be demonstrated that no amount of diversification can reduce the risk or the standard deviation of possible return beyond 74% of that of a one-stock portfolio. He states that, not only is the potential benefit from diversification fairly limited, but also a large part of this potential can be realized with a portfolio consisting of relatively few stocks.

Brealey's studies indicate that a portfolio of 20 stocks provides 94.2% of the advantages of diversification, and that each additional holding beyond 20 has a very negligible effect. For example, to increase the effect of diversification from 94.2% to 98.83%, the number of issues must increase from 20 to 100.[2] This will obviously increase costs and make the portfolio more difficult to manage.

Philosophy B advocates a portfolio of 20 or more low P/E-ratio stocks meeting certain quality criteria for financial soundness and stability and growth of shareholders' equity. (More will be said in chapter 10 about constructing and managing a portfolio of Philosophy B stocks. That chapter deals with the actual portfolio management process.)

Philosophy C

This is the most sophisticated of the philosophies, since it focuses on buying very good businesses at low prices. By buying at bargain prices the stocks of highly profitable businesses that are managed by good honest managers, the investor can feel that he is a part owner of a business, that he can prosper as the business prospers, and that he can compound his investment as the asset base of the companies increase. Only when the economics of the business change, the management changes, or the price moves out of line with the economic value of the company, does the investor need to sell his interest in that company. As a result, turnover is less, which reduces commissions, and taxes are postponed.

Here are some financial statistics for two different companies (see Table 7-2). From looking at these numbers, of which would you want to be a part owner?

In the first example, Company A, you will note that the book value, or asset value per share, increased from $57.78 to $69.65 over the five-year period, 1977-82. This is a yearly compound rate of 3.8%. During this same period, the number of shares grew from 647.63 million to 890 million, a yearly compound rate of 6.56%. The company was able to expand only through the injection of new capital and, even at that, its book value grew at a rate lower than the growth in number of shares. The cash flow from operations—earnings plus non-cash charges such as depreciation—was not enough to support the

Table 7-2.

Company A

	1977	1978	1979	1980	1981	1982
Sales per share	56.35	61.23	64.74	67.29	71.42	74.70
"Cash flow" per share...	14.52	15.91	16.61	17.18	17.96	18.30
Earnings per share	6.97	7.74	8.04	8.19	8.55	8.55
Div'ds decl'd per sh	4.20	4.60	5.00	5.00	5.40	5.40
Cap'l spending per sh ...	17.44	20.01	22.26	22.56	22.20	19.55
Book value per share ...	57.78	60.67	63.43	65.51	67.52	69.65
Common shs outst'	647.63	669.55	701.37	754.82	815.11	890.00
Avg ann'l P/E ratio	8.9	7.9	7.3	6.3	6.4	6.6
Avg ann'l earn's yield ...	11.2%	12.7%	13.7%	15.9%	15.6%	15.2%
Avg ann'l div'd yield	6.8%	7.6%	8.6%	9.7%	9.9%	9.6%

Company B

	1977	1978	1979	1980	1981	1982
Sales per share	66.01	68.14	88.23	99.46	112.04	115.50
"Cash flow" per share...	6.63	6.81	8.22	9.64	10.85	11.60
Earnings per share	4.36	4.51	5.23	6.23	7.08	7.15
Div'ds decl'd per sh	1.67	1.79	1.95	2.18	2.50	2.85
Cap'l spending per sh ...	2.95	3.95	6.76	8.63	7.38	9.00
Book value per share ...	23.27	25.97	29.10	32.96	37.63	43.10
Common shs outst'	96.40	97.18	101.27	104.10	104.35	112.50
Avg ann'l P/E ratio	7.5	6.4	5.7	6.1	6.6	6.5
Avg ann'l earn's yield ...	13.3%	15.6%	17.5%	16.4%	15.2%	15.5%
Avg ann'l div'd yield	5.1%	6.2%	6.5%	5.7%	5.4%	6.0%

Source: Company A—"American Telephone," *The Value Line Investment Survey,* January 28, 1983, p. 751.

Company B—"Reynolds Industries," *The Value Line Investment Survey,* January 7, 1983, p. 334.

company's capital spending programs, even before dividend payments were made to the owners. This indicates to us that the dividend on this company is, technically, a distribution of capital on which the investor pays taxes. He then must reinvest, after taxes, in more stock if he wishes to retain his proportionate ownership in the corporation.

Company B's book value from 1977-82 has grown at a 13% compound rate, while the number of shares outstanding have grown at a 3% compound rate. By taking the cash-flow figure from operations and subtracting the amounts for capital expenditures and dividends each year, you will find that the company generated excess cash flow of $2.14 per share over the five-year period. The dividend has grown at an 11.3% compound rate over that period and represents, in this case, a distribution of money from operations instead of from new capital subscriptions.

Given the two choices mentioned, of which company would you rather be an owner? If you chose Company B, you show an acuteness for selecting a good business while avoiding what is commonly known as an "investment." Company B is R. J. Reynolds Industries, a leader in what is probably the most profitable industry in the world, tobacco. Company A is one of the nation's most widely owned stocks, perceived to be a very conservative investment: American Telephone & Telegraph.

References

1. Sanjoy Basu, "Investment Performance of Common Stocks in Relation to their Price-Earnings Ratios: A Test of the Efficient Market Hypothesis," *Journal of Finance,* June 1977, pp. 663-682.
2. Richard Brealey, *An Introduction to Risk and Return From Common Stocks,* (Cambridge, Mass.: M.I.T. Press, 1969), pp. 125-128.

CHAPTER 8

Identifying High-Quality Companies for Long-Term Compounding

The final refinement of the basic low P/E-ratio philosophy advocated in this book centers on the selection of high-quality companies. The investor, when evaluating individual companies for investment, should consider three factors: one, the stock price; two, the economic characteristics of the company; and three, the management of the company. If all three factors are favorable, the investment has a high probability of providing above-average results over time.

The first of these factors, stock price, has been discussed earlier. It is the foundation of the three philosophies advocated here. The other two factors, economic characteristics of the business and management, complete the discussion needed to build the third philosophy.

It is our contention that an investment in a business with certain economic characteristics — acquired at the right price and managed with the owners' interest in mind — will provide above-average returns to the investor's portfolio, while reducing portfolio turnover, hence commissions and taxes.

Now, recall the importance of compounding in the investment process and how bonds serve as a benchmark for establishing a standard of value. Given a combination of time and high interest rates, the reinvestment of income to receive additional income—interest on interest—can lead to the accumulation of large sums of money. This income flows to the investor with only two costs, taxes and inflation. As we said, the investor can minimize these costs through proper planning. The income left after taxes and inflation can be used to acquire more income-producing assets to continue the compounding process.

Unfortunately, during the inflationary economic environment that has prevailed during the 1970s and early 1980s, the profits reported to shareholders by many large corporations have been, in part, real earnings and, in part, illusion. Often, if one considers the cost of replacement of worn-out plants and equipment and the inventories used to generate the sales from which the profits were derived, the reported profits of many corporations on which taxes and dividends were paid did not actually exist.

The investor's first step in the selection of a good company in which to invest is to find a company that reports actual earnings that are a function of its operations, not a result of inflation, accounting gimmickry, or tax-rate manipulation. The problem in measuring earnings using historical cost accounting, as our economic system does, has been recognized for some time. David F. Hawkins, accounting consultant for Drexel Burnham, states the problem in "Drexel Burnham Accounting Bulletin No. 3," May 1974, as follows:

> One definition of profits in economic theory states that you have *not* earned a profit until you have earned enough to replace that which you sold. Price-level accounting does not produce an income figure that is consistent with this economic concept. The principal reason for this inconsistency is that the cost of goods sold and depreciation expense reported in price-level statements is an expression of the purchasing power equivalent in current dollars of the original historical dollar cost of the asset acquired. This dollar number does not necessarily measure the current replacement cost of the asset consumed.
>
> In the case of a going concern that is trying to grow in real terms, unless it earns enough purchasing power to replace the assets sold it has not created a source of funds from operations that will keep its growth going. Just recovering the original purchasing power invested in the asset consumed is not enough, if the current purchasing

power required to replace the consumed item is greater than this amount (p. 13).

More recently, in an article appearing in *Forbes* entitled "Are More Chryslers in the Offing?"[2] Richard Greene discusses the problems facing many industrial corporations that, in an era of high inflation, calculate profits by use of an accounting system based on historical cost figures. He writes:

> Although the trend is toward faster depreciation there are still a fair number of firms that don't want to punish earnings that way. So, they keep their depreciation nice and slow and earnings nice and high. This is a perfect formula for earnings success if you don't mind rusting plants, inferior R&D and yesterday's technology.

> All of this adds up to some rather jarring differences between the picture of a company as seen through earnings analysis and the status of a firm discovered through attention to cash flow.

> Take a look, for example, at Dow Chemical and Union Carbide, two giant chemical companies. Over the four years from 1976 to 1979, Dow showed earnings totaling about $2.5 billion. Over the same period, Union Carbide reported cumulative earnings of some $1.8 billion. It would appear that both firms were robust money-makers in the same league.

> But take it a step further and look at cash flow. Kidder, Peabody & Co. did this and, although Kidder's methodology is a bit controversial, the question is a matter of degree — not direction. Kidder came up with a number called discretionary cash flow. That's the figure representing how much money a firm has left to grow with — after taking out the amount necessary to maintain its property, plant and equipment after dividends. Companies don't really set aside money to replace equipment but ultimately they have to put out that cash — and it's not going toward growth.

> Dow's discretionary cash flow is at a healthy level, with $924 million over the four-year period. But Union Carbide has a different story, negative discretionary cash flow of $663 million. That means according to Kidder, UC was paying dividends for that whole period of time with borrowed money. It was, in effect, cannibalizing its capital structure to keep the stock price up. That's not a healthy habit. But it's common among the kind of huge firms you'd think would

know better. Kidder's list only begins with U.S. Steel, Bethlehem Steel, American Can, Goodyear, and Inco.

Greene includes the results of a study done by Barre W. Littel and Robert Levine of Kidder, Peabody & Company. These results show some rather interesting and revealing examples of major United States corporations that are not generating actual profits.

The awful truth

"The extent to which major corporations are neglecting their plant and equipment, and paying dividends with cash they don't have, becomes painfully clear by looking at cash flow.

"Kidder, Peabody & Co. recently calculated cash-flow numbers for 20 of the 30 companies that make up the Dow Jones Industrial Average. Although many people think of cash flow as a simple addition of pretax earnings and depreciation, Kidder goes a giant step further. It recalculates the depreciation figure to take into account the ravages of inflation on historical depreciation schedules.

"With this adjustment, 11 of the 20 companies came out of Kidder's computer with negative distributable cash flow for 1980. (That's the number showing how much money a firm really has control over, to spend on either growth or dividends.) On a cumulative basis for 1975 to 1979, 8 of these firms showed negative distributable cash flow.

"You'd think that companies with negative distributable cash flow wouldn't continue giving dividends. Not so. In fact, the discretionary cash flow figure— distributable cash flow minus dividends—shows that 14 of these firms were paying dividends in 1980 with cash that, by Kidder's hard test, they do not have.

"Some firms, of course, may be letting their plants run down deliberately—in effect, liquidating those assets—preparing to move into new, more lucrative businesses. But such decisions in specific cases hardly explain away the broadly negative results of Kidder's calculations."

We believe that an owner in a private business thinks in terms of cash flow, not merely in terms of earnings. Most investors in publicly held corporations concentrate on changes in earnings. Alcoa, an institutional favorite, has not earned any "real profits" in five years. As can be seen in Table 8-1, the same is true for many other highly capitalized companies.

One key indicator that can separate the actual earners from the masses is the concept of "net free cash flow" observed over a period of several years.

Table 8-1. Major U.S. corporations' actual profit generating capacity.

Company	1980 Net income (est.)	1980 Distributable cash flow	1980 Discretionary cash flow	1975-79 Net income as reported	1975-79 Distributable cash flow	1975-79 Discretionary cash flow
Alcoa	445.0	$ 58.3	$ − 57.7	$1,221.1	$ − 185.4	$ − 493.9
American Brands .	389.0	184.3	42.1	978.6	495.4	− 29.1
American Can . . .	95.7	− 165.7	− 225.5	533.7	− 141.6	− 390.6
Bethlehem Steel . .	95.0	− 399.2	− 469.2	462.6	−1,660.8	− 2,082.0
Du Pont	670.0	− 35.3	− 455.3	2,997.6	1,016.1	− 517.0
General Electric . .	1,490.0	852.4	152.4	5,345.8	3,396.6	906.8
General Foods . . .	262.0[1]	133.8	23.9	985.1	146.5	− 268.8
General Motors . .	− 880.0	− 4,069.1	− 4,947.1	13,894.1	5,393.5	− 2,127.6
Goodyear	169.0	− 488.2	− 581.3	861.7	−1,144.4	− 1,445.3
Inco	200.0	− 86.5	− 166.5	646.3	−515.6	− 986.6
IBM	3,500.0	5,390.6	3,390.6	13,229.3	19,500.5	11,972.1
International Harvester	− 397.3[2]	− 984.9	− 1,030.9	1,085.1	−179.8	− 475.1
Johns-Manville . . .	73.2	− 51.2	− 119.2	430.6	46.5	− 140.7
Merck	431.0	293.8	113.8	1,451.1	1,056.2	446.2
Owens-Illinois . . .	127.3	2.8	− 40.7	528.0	− 16.7	− 184.7
Procter & Gamble	642.8[3]	319.5	38.4	2,285.5	1,455.2	425.4
Sears, Roebuck . . .	475.0[4]	− 220.6	− 649.6	3,786.6	1,272.5	− 437.0
Union Carbide . . .	885.3	− 154.4	− 360.4	2,158.5	30.8	− 819.6
U.S. Steel	353.0	− 1,333.7	− 1,472.7	673.4	−4,883.1	− 6,622.6
United Technologies . . .	390.0	96.4	− 79.6	1,030.6	694.1	264.5

Note: All dollar figures in millions.
1. Year ending March 1981.
2. As reported year ending October 1980.
3. As reported year ending June 1980.
4. Year ending January 1981.

Source: Richard Greene, "Are More Chryslers in the Offing?" p. 71.

The investor should calculate cash flow from operations, i.e., earnings plus non-cash charges such as depreciation, and subtract from this number all dividends and capital expenditures. If the figure is positive over a period of time, the most recent five years, the company probably does not face too much of a problem of reporting inflated profits.

To illustrate these problems of the quality of earnings and of the use of the cash-flow calulation, we'll give and explain several examples using various stock market indices or averages. There are three different levels of sophistication in this exercise. The first is the basic cash-flow analysis easily obtained from The Value Line Investment Survey. Here the authors use the Value Line Industrial Composite.

Table 8-2. Basic cash flow analysis of The Value Line Industrial Composite.

	1963-67	1968-72	1973-77
Cash flow per share	$ 11.09	$ 15.72	$ 17.61
Less dividends per share	$ 3.63	$ 4.31	$ 3.94
Less capital spending per share	$ 8.32	$ 12.62	14.61
Equals free cash flow	$ −0.86	$ −1.21	$ −0.94

	1978	1979	1980	1981	1982	1978-1982
Cash flow per share	$ 4.76	$ 5.98	$ 6.17	$ 6.27	$ 5.70	$ 22.88
Less dividends per share	$ 1.07	$ 1.23	$ 1.36	$ 1.43	$ 1.45	$ 6.54
Less Capital spending per share	$ 3.88	$ 5.02	$ 5.92	$ 6.70	$ 6.60	$ 28.12
Equals free cash flow	$ −.19	$ −.27	$ −1.11	$ −1.86	$ −2.35	$ −5.78

Source: Value Line Inc., "Selections & Opinions," *Value Line 900 Industrial Composite,* February 25, 1983, p. 433.

Using the same method, we present the Financial Dynamics' Composite of the companies in the Standard & Poor's 400 Industrials from Standard & Poor's Compustat Services, Inc., also readily available.

Table 8-3. Basic cash-flow analysis of the Standard & Poor's 400 Industrial Composite.*

	1972-76
Cash flow	$ 363.45
Less dividends	$ 87.95
Less capital spending	$ 308.29
Equals free cash flow	$ − 32.79

(billions)	1977	1978	1979	1980	1981	1977-81
Cash flow	$ 98.81	$ 113.10	$ 138.37	$ 150.01	$ 165.23	$ 665.52
Less dividends .	$ 24.88	$ 27.38	$ 30.64	$ 34.86	$ 38.78	$ 156.54
Less capital spending	$ 82.52	$ 95.90	$ 119.92	$ 146.36	$ 168.22	$ 612.92
Equals free cash flow . . .	$ − 8.59	$ − 10.18	$ − 12.19	$ − 31.21	$ − 41.77	$ −103.94

* Based on December 31, 1981 Standard & Poor's 400 population.

Source: *Standard & Poor's Compustat Services, Inc.* "Financial Dynamics Standard & Poor's 400 Industrial Composite," 1982.

Both of these composite indices show excellent statistical cross sections of American industry. The findings confirm what has been discussed. The articles cited point out the problems faced by American corporations of under depreciation of assets, of inventory valuation, and of lack of high, real earning power to cover the true working capital needs for sales increases by the corporations. The Value Line Industrial Composite shows, numerically, the deterioration of cash-flow coverage of capital spending and dividends.

Table 8-4. Basic cash-flow analysis of the Value Line Industrial Composite.

	1963-67	1968-72	1973-77	1978-82
Cash flow per share	$ 11.09	$ 15.72	$ 17.61	$ 28.88
Less dividends per share . .	$ 3.63	$ 4.31	$ 3.94	$ 6.54
Less capital spending per share	$ 8.32	$ 12.62	$ 14.61	$ 28.12
Equals free cash flow	$ − 0.86	$ − 1.21	$ − 0.94	$ − 5.78

Source: Value Line Inc., "Selections and Opinions," *Value Line 900 Industrial Composite,* 1977, 1981, 1983.

The Standard & Poor's 400 Industrial Composite shows the same trends resulting in a deterioration of the cash-flow coverage of dividends and capital spending. Basically, American corporations are not earning enough internally to cover their capital expenditures, maintenance, upgrading, and replacement and expansion and their dividends.

Table 8-5. Basic cash flow analysis of the Standard & Poor's 400 Industrial Composite.

	1972-76	1977-81
Cash flow	$ 363.45	$ 665.52
Less dividend	$ 87.95	$ 156.54
Less capital spending	$ 308.29	$ 612.92
Equals free cash flow	$ – 32.79	$ – 103.94

Source: *Standard & Poor's Compustat Services, Inc.*, "Financial Dynamics Standard & Poor's 400 Industrial Composite," 1982.

Some practitioners might consider this to be a rather simplified approach to a complicated problem, but it does demonstrate that American corporations are in a period of liquidation. The dollars get bigger, but the shareholder gets poorer. He gets poorer because cash flows are inadequate to support the business. This requires the investor to subscribe to more stock or to purchase bonds, thereby providing an infusion of needed cash to the corporation. If negative cash flow was a one- or two-year phenomenon and then reverted to positive cash flow, there would be no real problem. But, as can be seen, this problem has been present for some time and has worsened as inflation has increased.

There are two exceptions to consider in the above approach. The first is that the free cash-flow figure, whether positive or negative, can give a false signal. A company that fails to maintain its plant and has a lower-than-needed capital spending program may appear to have a positive free cash flow. Over time, a company that continually fails to meet its capital requirements will eventually see its profitability fall as plant and equipment deteriorate.

Contrarily, a company with a temporarily negative free cash flow may not be all bad if the reason is a current increase in capital spending for expansion purposes. This points out the importance of viewing the figures over several years.

The second exception is that the above figures may be optimistic, that the true situation may be worse than shown. It is beyond the scope of this book to give a detailed financial analysis of this problem, but a brief mention of three more-sophisticated approaches is in order.

The first approach is called the "net cash flow from operations," described by Leopold A. Bernstein in his book *Financial Statement Analysis*.[3] Bernstein writes:

> Analytically, the most useful way to compute Net Cash Flow from Operations (NCFO) is to show the elements of revenue that generate cash and the expenses that use cash (the "inflow-outflow" approach) rather than to adjust net income for noncash affecting items (the "net" approach).

> The first step is to identify and list all elements of income and expense *that affect* working capital. The second step is to adjust them for changes in *working capital items* (other than cash) which are *assumed* to affect operations. Thus:

A. Starting with sales
    + Decrease (− increase) in accounts receivable

    = Cash collections on sales
    + Other revenues (+ or − adjustments for noncash items)

    = Total cash collections from operations

B. Cost of goods sold (excluding depreciation, amortization, etc.)
    + Increase (− decrease) in inventories
    + Decrease (− increase) in trade payables
    + Operating Expenses (SG&A)
    + Other Expenses (including interest)
    + Increase (− decrease) in prepaid assets
    + Decrease (− increase) in accrued liabilities
    + Income Tax Expense (excluding deferred taxes-noncurrent)
    + Decrease (− increase) in accrued taxes

    = Deduct total cash *outflows for* operations

$A - B$ = Net cash flows from operations (NCFO).

This is a truer picture of cash flow for comparison to capital spending and dividend payments. This method takes into account the changes in working capital rather than capital spending alone.

The second approach is called "cash flow provided by operations," which is described by James A. Largay III and Clyde P. Stickney in *Financial Analysts Journal,* July-August 1980, titled "Cash Flows, Ratio Analysis and the W. T. Grant Company Bankruptcy."[4] Largay and Stickney discuss both the problems with the use of traditional cash-flow numbers and the benefit of the use of cash flow from operations. They write:

> The most striking characteristic of the Grant Company during the decade before its bankruptcy was that it generated virtually no cash internally. The company simply lost its ability to derive cash from operations. After exhausting the possibilities of its liquid resources, it had to tap external markets for funds. As the failure to generate cash internally continued the need for external financing snowballed.

> Most textbooks in corporate finance, investments and financial statement analysis devote little attention to computing or using cash flow from operations. Yet the calculations are straight-forward enough. One starts with working capital provided by operations from the statement of changes in financial position, adds changes in current asset accounts (other than cash) that decreased and current liability accounts that increased and subtracts changes in current asset accounts (other than cash) that increased and current liability accounts that decreased. In accounting terms, the calculation is equivalent to adding credit changes in working capital accounts and subtracting debit changes. Chart 8-1 summarizes the process of converting working capital provided by operations to cash flow provided by operations (p. 186).

Chart 8-1. Computing cash flow provided by operations from published financial statements.

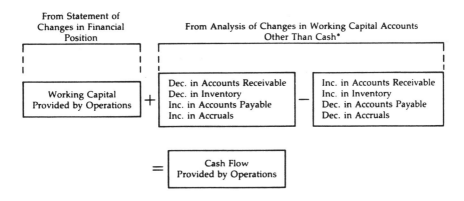

*Accounts such as "Bank Loans" and "Current Portion of Long-Term Debt" must be excluded from the analysis. Even though treated as current liabilities, they represent neither cash provided nor cash used by operations.

Source: Largay and Stickney, "Cash Flows, Ratio Analysis and the W. T. Grant Company Bankruptcy."

Now that "cash flow provided by operations" has been calculated, what does it actually indicate in the example of the W. T. Grant Company? Largay and Stickney continue.

> Chart 8-2 graphs Grant's net income, working capital provided by oeprations and cash flow provided by operations for the 1966 to 1975 fiscal periods. Note how poorly working capital provided by operations correlates with cash flow from operations. The financial press frequently refers to "cash flow," defined as net income plus depreciation. This measure of cash flow approximates working capital provided by operations, which (as Chart 8-2 shows) may prove a very poor surrogate for the cash flow actually generated by operations. While Grant's net income was relatively steady through the 1973 period, operations were a net user, rather than provider, of cash in all but two years (1968 and 1969). Even in these two years, operations provided only insignificant amounts of cash. Grant's continuing inability to generate cash from operations should have provided investors with an early signal of problems (p. 186).

**Chart 8-2. W. T. Grant Company Net Income, Working Capital and
Cash Flow From Operations for Fiscal Years Ending January 31, 1966 to 1975.**

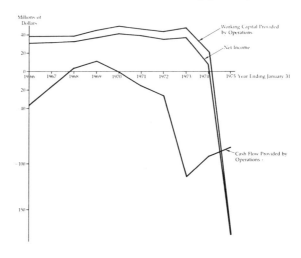

Source: Largay and Stickney, p. 187.

Obviously, "cash flow from operations" is very important. All American corporations do not represent situations comparable to that of the W. T. Grant Company, but many individual companies might.

The third, and most sophisticated, of the three approaches is "excess cash flow." This approach was originated by Barre W. Littel in 1975. In a paper titled "Financial Quality Profile—Introduction to FQP Theory, Ratios and Scoring," December 19, 1980, Littel and Levine described Littel's approach:[5]

Excess Cash Flow Defined
The objective of the Excess Cash Flow technique is to identify total annual funds (if any) available to finance a business. The method used is to develop for each company a consistent, conservative "set of books," which, among other things, standardizes accounting methods and requires the adjustment of reported figures for the distortions of inflation. The "centerpiece" of our analytical system is what we call the Excess Cash Flow approach. In short, the Excess Cash Flow technique deducts from traditional cash flow (1) inventory profits (for companies not on LIFO), (2) depreciation of fixed

assets at current cost and at a standardized economic life appropriate for a company's industry, (3) general inflation in receivables less payables and accruals, and (4) dividends; it adds back incremental borrowing capacity (trendline borrowing). (Littel and Levine, p. 3.)

This method is unique because it looks at the true economic world of corporate finances, gives the user a "real earnings" number, and calculates a fundable unit growth or real growth for the company in question. If the Value Line Industrial Composite or the Standard and Poor's 400 Industrial Composite were measured against Littel's model, the deterioration of America's corporations would probably appear to be worse than it appeared from the calculation of the less-sophisticated examples. Littel's "excess cash flow/unit growth fundable" model is calculated as shown in Table 8-6.

Table 8-6. Computation of excess cash flow and unit growth fundable.

1.		Cash flow (net income plus depreciation plus deferred taxes)
2.	Minus:	Inventory valuation adjustment (IVA) before taxes
3.	Minus:	Capital expenditures required to maintain productive capability
4.	Minus:	(General inflation in receivables less payables and accruals)
5.	Equals:	*Distributable cash flow*
6.	Minus:	Dividends paid
7.	Equals:	*Discretionary cash flow*
8.	Plus:	Incremental borrowing capacity
9.	Equals:	*Excess cash flow*
10.	Divided by:	Updated net assets employed in the business
11.	Equals:	*Unit growth fundable*

Source: Littel and Levine, p. 3.

Armed with Littel and Levine's analysis of a company, an investor can ask some pointed questions before he invests his funds. The answer to these questions can lead an investor to invest in the corporate "winners" and leave the "losers" alone.

If the prices of the corporate "winners" are too high, the alternative invest-ment of funds in short-term to intermediate-term bonds of high quality may be preferred. The cash from the bond is subject to inflation and taxes, not to inflation, taxes, underdepreciation of assets, lack of adequate working capital, and a host of other variables.

Why is it that some companies are able to grow in real terms so that their owners' wealth increases? What are the characteristics of "good companies" that lead to a high "real return on equity" or "real growth" per share? To set the stage for a listing of the characteristics of a good company, one has to understand the process by which a company increases its shareholders' equity. We will explain this process and show how these characteristics of a good com-pany affect the rate of growth of shareholders' equity.

Table 8-7.
A. Standard income profit-and-loss statement

Sales (price × units)
     − Cost of goods sold
          Labor and related expense
          Pension and retirement expense
          Materials
     = Gross income (gross margins)
     − Selling, general, and administrative expenses, research/marketing
     = Operating income before depreciation (operating margins)
     − Depreciation depletion and amortization
     = Operating income after depreciation
  +/− Other (income or expense net)
     − Interest expense
     = Pre-tax income (pre-tax profit margins)
     − Income taxes
     = After-tax income (after-tax profit margins)
     − Preferred dividends
     = Net income (net income margin)

B. Calculation of growth of stockholders' equity.

Net income:
     ÷ Beginning-year stockholders' equity
     = Return on stockholders' equity
     × Retention rate (net income − dividend)
     = Growth of stockholders' equity

Section A presents the components of the income statement, and Section B shows the effect of net income on stockholders' equity. What is retained—or not paid out in the form of dividends—increases stockholders' equity. This increase can be expressed as a percentage, which is the growth rate of the stockholders' equity.

The key to investment success is to buy stock in a company whose return-on-equity remains in a high range and to buy it at a price as close as possible to stockholders' equity, i.e., book value. This results in buying a stock at a low P/E ratio. Let's consider some of the positive characteristics to consider in selection of a stock for investment.

The positive characteristics that affect sales (price multiplied by units) are:

1. Pricing power is the single most important characteristic. This is the ability to raise prices, to retain margins and profitability, even in poor economic times when unit volume may be flat and capacity may not be fully utilized. As a company's costs rise, the degree to which the company can pass on these cost increases will determine its ability to sustain its return on equity. Most markets, however, are highly competitive. The needed price increases, therefore, cannot be put into effect.

In contrast, the company with pricing power can pass on its cost increases and can retain profitability without losing business. To accomplish this, a company must have a unique economic position. Companies that offer unique, high-quality goods or services (where the service is more significant to the customer than the cost), or companies that are in oligolopistic market situations like those in the tobacco industry (where the threat of new entrants is low), have this economic position.

A company must be able to raise prices without attracting political opposition, regulation, import competition, new entrants, or threats of product substitution. Few, if any, companies will have all the characteristics that lead to flexible pricing. But some can come close, for example, newspapers and tobacco firms.

We think that pricing power is the most important characteristic of all the characteristics of "good companies." As can be seen from Table 8-7, a company that retains pricing power has a much greater chance to earn an above-average return on its invested capital and an above-average return on shareholders' equity.

2. Unit growth is an important component of the sales formula, but is probably greatly over-rated. Most investors will focus on companies with above-average growth in unit volume. These are classified as "growth industries" or "growth companies," and there is fierce competition, via stock price, among

investors for these high-unit-growth companies.

Moreover, a short-term financial benefit occurs when a company with excess or unused capacity increases its unit production and operates at full capacity. As the units of production rise with a fixed asset base, overhead costs and all fixed expenses fall as a percentage of sales, because these costs fall on a per-unit basis. Thus, the profitability rises dramatically in some cases.

We believe that unit growth is important, but not as important as pricing power. It is important to realize that a business with pricing power but no unit growth can still provide a high or above-average return on stockholders' equity. The portion of this above-average return that is retained (i.e., not paid out in dividends) can be invested in new businesses through acquisitions paid for in cash, or by starting new companies. We focus on the ability to sustain the returns on capital, rather than on growth in earnings per share.

The characteristics of good companies that affect the cost of goods sold are:

1. Cost flexibility can keep costs from rising rapidly, enabling companies to maintain profit margins and to limit their increases in the prices of their products. This cost flexibility can be accomplished in many ways. Companies that use many suppliers rather than only one can negotiate among suppliers. Companies that constitute a large percentage of a supplier's sales can negotiate with that supplier. Using materials that have many substitutes will enable the user to negotiate costs by threatening to use substitutes.[6]

2. Low cost of labor in relation to sales is a positive characteristic. When this relationship exists, labor demands can be met more easily. Costs can be passed on in the form of higher prices for products. The ability to avert strikes and labor disruptions is important. Highly skilled employees or unionized labor can exert tremendous pressures on costs. Also, the difficulty of finding highly skilled labor would tend to inhibit expansion.[7]

3. Pension and retirement expenses are becoming a larger and larger expense for labor-intensive businesses. The smart investor looks for companies with low labor costs and with adequately funded pension plans. Unfunded pension liabilities should be viewed negatively because these liabilities must be met in the future before any claims by equity owners.

4. Inventories of a company consist of raw materials, work in progress, and finished goods. The cost of goods sold is affected by the method of inventory valuation, FIFO (first in first out), or LIFO (last in first out). In inflationary times, inventory valuations are constantly rising. If a company uses either FIFO or average cost, it reports illusory profits that are taxed, because the company has to replace its inventories at higher prices.

Under LIFO inventory accounting, a company generally does not report inventory profits caused by inflation. These companies have a higher cash flow because they don't pay taxes on inventory profits. A business that can use and replace its inventory frequently, and/or does not need much inventory for production, has many advantages. First, it doesn't tie up funds for items stored for future sales; second, it reduces the risk of maintaining an inventory of products that may become obsolete.

The good characteristics that affect selling, general, and administrative expenses are,

1. Companies that have flexibility in their expenses for advertising, research and development, and marketing and consumer incentives (such as coupons) can cut these costs quickly to offset other rising costs during periods of weak demand. This can be dangerous, though, if it results in losing sales in the future (Hawkins, p. 16).

2. For most people, research and development expenses represent a positive factor. But the investor should regard this expense from a different perspective. Research and development expenses are considered to be necessary for development of new proprietary products that will have a unique position in the market place and that will be able to earn an above-average rate of return.

In some cases, this actually occurs. But, in many cases, it does not. For example, R&D for the electronic computer industry creates new products that move through the market place at a rapid pace. An entire product cycle can occur over a 12- to 18-month period. Then, as high profitability begins to be generated from this new product, fierce competition, both in prices and in new features, arises among companies manufacturing the product. A healthy portion of the profits are spent to update the product. Because a company in the electronics industry without research and development would soon be out of business, the expenditure is not voluntary. It is necessary for survival.

Usually, the survivors in highly competitive industries that are dependent on research and development are large, well-established companies that have tremendous economies of scale. The occasional product breakthrough, e.g., Tagamet for Smithkline Beckman Company, is more a matter of chance than a foreseen event. (The chance event was the investment in Smithkline's stock when most drug analysts on Wall Street were not recommending it.)

Research and development expense is a good characteristic of a company if it increases the growth rate of the company with an above-average rate of return on assets. Mandatory expenditures on research and development, merely to stay competitive, are a negative characteristic.

The good characteristics that affect depreciation, depletion, and amortization expenses are:

1. Companies should have a low, fixed-cost base. This is calculated as a ratio of sales to each dollar of average gross plant value. If a company has a low fixed-cost base or high sales-to-gross-plant-value, depreciation charges will be a low percentage of sales. As costs rise, the price of capital equipment rises. When a company wants to expand a product line or to replace worn-out equipment, the cost will be greater than what the company has taken in depreciation. This effect will reduce the company's ability to grow, in real terms, because the company will have to spend much of its cash-flow to replace old plant facilities. There will be less, or possibly nothing, available for real growth. When fixed costs are low and depreciation is a smaller percentage of sales, cost increases for capital goods can be more easily passsed on as price increases. Table 8-8 demonstrates this point.

Table 8-8.

1982 Data	Sales per $1 Average Gross Plant Value	Depreciation as % of Sales
Standard & Poor's 400 Industrial Composite	$1.55	4.0
General Foods Corporation	3.62	1.6
Washington Post Company	3.10	3.8
American Home Products Corporation	4.21	1.6
American Tel. & Tel. Corporation	0.43	13.4

Source: *Standard & Poor's Compustat Services, Inc.,* "Financial Dynamics Annual Financial Analysis (various company documents) and Standard & Poor's 400 Industrial Composite" 1982.

General Foods Corporation, Washington Post Company, and American Home Products Corporation can cover cost increases for capital goods for expansion or replacement more easily than those American corporations represented by the Standard & Poor's 400 Industrial Composite. Given the above figures, imagine what is happening to American Telephone & Telegraph Company.

2. Companies should be conservative with their depreciation charges. Several methods of depreciation and different accounting life-expectancies assigned to equipment are used by different companies. The methods used by Dow Chemical Company and Union Carbide Corporation are examples.

Dow Chemical Company calculates depreciation by using the declining-balance method, while Union Carbide Corporation uses the straight-line depreciation method. Dow Chemical uses the figure of 11 years as useful plant life; Union Carbide uses 17 years. The income statement differences are presented in Table 8-9 below.

Table 8-9.

1982 Data	Union Carbide Corporation	Dow Chemical Company	Dow Chemical Adjusted
Sales	$9,061	$10,618	$10,618
Depreciation	426	879	499
Depreciation as % of sales	4.7%	8.2%	4.7%
Pre-tax income	$ 385	$ 356	$ 727

Source: *Annual Reports*, Dow Chemical Company and Union Carbide Corporation, 1982.

Union Carbide's depreciation is 4.7% of sales compared to Dow Chemical's 8.2%. If Dow Chemical calculated its depreciation by Union Carbide's method, Dow Chemical's pre-tax earnings would have increased by $371 million or 104%. Thus, conservative depreciation is a good characteristic of a company.

Good characteristics that influence interest expense are,

1. Companies that need very little or no external financing can wait to borrow at advantageous times and rates. Companies with low debt shown on their balance sheets will generally have lower borrowing costs and more financial flexibility.

2. Because of the deductibility of interest costs, companies employ long-term leverage to increase their return on shareholders' equity. A good company is one that can earn an above-average return on shareholders' equity without debt, or at least with very little debt. Many companies have below-average interest costs imbedded in their balance sheets, but the old debts are rapidly maturing. When a company replaces this debt, the interest costs rise substantially.

A good characteristic is for a company to have a full tax rate. For 1981, the Standard & Poor's 400 Industrial Composite's tax rate was 43%; the Value Line Industrial Composite's rate was 46%. If a company has a lower-than-average tax rate, the reasons for that rate should be known. (This is usually explained in the footnotes of the annual report.) If the rate rises in subsequent years, the after-tax earnings to the investor will probably be reduced. This reduction will lower his after-tax return on invested capital.

Other good characteristics related to the income statement shown in the earnings model are:

1. Preferred stock, in our opionion, is very similar to a bond with no maturity date. Preferred stock has a significant disadvantage in that the issuing company cannot deduct interest expense and dividend payments for tax purposes. Any company that issues a lot of preferred stock should be avoided.

2. An excellent business is one that provides a product or service that customers either enjoy very much or find practically indispensable and for which the customer can find no substitutes. As a result, sales are less subject to business-cycle fluctuations and to competitors' strategies.

Taken collectively, these good characteristics enable a company to achieve high income in relation to its invested capital. To complete the equation for the calculation of the investor's return, the investor should focus on the company's balance sheet. Better companies will have low levels of debt in relation to stockholders' equity. A low level of debt and the reduced level of borrowing needs will generally make a company less vulnerable to periods of tight credit and will always provide more alternatives for future financing needs. A company with a low level of debt can manage its balance of debt by choice, particularly if the company is self-financing.

The aforementioned good company characteristics, shown on its balance sheet and income statement, lead to above-average returns on the company's invested capital. It is from these high returns that the investor benefits.

1. A high or above-average, sustainable return on stockholders' equity, even though it may fluctuate, is the key characteristic of a good company that benefits the investor. Return on stockholders' equity is the component that builds shareholders' wealth. It is a focal point for the investor.

In Table 8-7, the relationship between net income (as shown on the income statement) and stockholders' equity (as shown on the balance sheet) becomes clear. Net income divided by stockholders' equity at the beginning of the year equals return on stockholders' equity. Net income less dividends is called retained earnings. The retained earnings for the year are added to the stockholders' equity for the beginning of the year. Now the company is worth more because it has more stockholders' equity or book value. This increase in stockholders' equity becomes capital used to fund added growth and to increase the owners' wealth.

2. A high and sustainable return — again, even though it fluctuates, is a good characteristic. Return on total assets is a truer measure of management's ability than is return on equity. Peter F. Drucker in an article, "Measuring Business Performance," states,

> . . .The demand for full disclosure increasingly focuses on the economic prospects of a company and on its economic performance — that is, on the extent to which it actually produces wealth out of the resources entrusted to it.

> The key figure for this is return on all assets (or on capital employed), related to cash needs, to cost of capital, to risk and needs. . . And it is this figure that should provide the link between business performance and executive compensation.[8]

There are several ways to calculate return on total assets. The most common is to divide the sum of net income plus 50% of the interest charges on long-term debt by total capital.[9] This is the Value Line Investment Survey method. Standard & Poor's Compustat Services, Inc.'s Financial Dynamics Industrial Service calculates a return on assets by dividing net income, before extraordinary items, by average total assets.[10] In Drucker's article, return on total assets is calculated by dividing the sum of net income plus all interest on all debt plus depreciation by total assets, or total capital, employed in the business.[11] (We prefer total assets rather than total capital.) This calculation should be done for a period of several years.

3. A "high plowback ratio" or high "unit growth fundable" is a good characteristic that relates to the actual growth of a company. Again, this measure relates the balance sheet to the income statement. These ratios were discussed earlier when we were describing how America's corporations were liquidating themselves and pointing to the need to find companies that produced real earnings after real depreciation costs, inventories, and other costs.

A simple method of calculating the "plowback ratio" is stated by O'Conner, Hersch, and Otis at the Fourteen Research Corporation in New York.[12] The figure is called the "cash plowback ratio." It is calculated as follows: Net income plus depreciation minus dividends is then divided by gross plant plus net working capital plus investments plus other assets at the beginning of the year. The "cash plowback ratio" was developed by the chemical industry to measure financial self-sufficiency and the reinvestment rates of funds to support long-term growth.

O'Conner, Hersch, and Otis found that a "cash plowback ratio" of 8% is needed to sustain additions to working capital, in inflationary terms, and to replace obsolete facilities. The Dow Jones Industrial Average cash plowback is about 6%, and the Standard & Poor's 400 Industrial Composite ratio is about 8.5%. From this it can be seen that the Dow Jones Industrial Average's earnings are not high enough to support its capital spending and dividends, and that the Standard & Poor's Industrial Composite is merely keeping up. American Telephone & Telegraph Company's plowback ratio is about 7%, while R. J. Reynolds Industries' is 11%. This method is sufficient for a quick approximation of a company's financial condition.

The preferred, but most complicated, method is Kidder, Peabody & Company's "Excess Cash Flow." Littel, who originated the method, discussed it in a Kidder, Peabody & Company report, "Excess Cash Flow Analysis."[13] The benefits in Kidder's approach were,

1. Adjustments were made to cash-flow figures for inventory profits of companies not using the LIFO method of accounting.

2. Adjustments were made for underdepreciation of fixed assets for various companies.

3. Adjustment was made for the general inflation in working capital needed to maintain the current level of business.

4. Adjustment was made for the incremental borrowing capacity as the stockholders' equity grows.

The most important adjustment so far as we are concerned is for underdepreciation of fixed assets and general inflation of working capital. The Kidder, Peabody and Company "Excess Cash Flow" formula is outlined in Table 8-10.

After these adjustments to cash flow—net income plus depreciation plus deferred taxes—the company's real growth potential is revealed. The investor should look for companies that have above-average "Excess Cash Flow and unit growth fundable."

With a combination of good characteristics affecting section A, the income statement, and section B, the balance sheet, of the company model referred to in Tables 8-7, the company can be classified as a "corporate winner" or "real earner." A corporate winner or real earner will increase shareholder equity per share at an above-average rate in real or inflation-adjusted terms. One reminder: These stocks must be purchased at the right price.

Table 8-10. Computation of excess cash flow and unit growth fundable.

1.		Cash flow (net income plus depreciation plus deferred taxes)
2.	Minus:	Inventory valuation adjustment (IVA) before taxes
3.	Minus:	Capital expenditures required to maintain productive capability
4.	Minus:	(General inflation in receivables less payables and accruals)
5.	Equals:	*Disbributable cash flow*
6.	Minus:	Dividends Paid
7.	Equals:	*Discretionary cash flow*
8.	Plus:	Incremental borrowing capacity
9.	Equals:	*Excess cash flow*
10.	Divided by:	Updated net assets employed in the business
11.	Equals:	*Unit growth fundable*

Source: Littel and Levine, "Financial Quality Profile," p. 3.

Table 8-11. Companies' internal growth rates and return on stockholders' equity.

1981 Data	Standard & Poor's 400 Industrials	R. J. Reynolds	American Telephone & Telegraph	Nabisco Brands, Inc.	General Foods Corp.
Sales per $ avg tot assets	1.35	1.26	0.44	2.31	2.39
× Pretax margin	8.8%	14.3%	19.3%	8.2%	5.0%
= P/T ret on avg tot assets	11.8%	18.1%	8.6%	18.9%	11.9%
× Retention rate (AT Inc/PT Inc)	0.56	0.55	0.61	0.56	0.53
= A/T ret on avg tot assets	6.7%	9.9%	5.2%	10.6%	6.3%
− Preferred dividend factor	0.1%	0.4%	0.1%	0.0%	0.0%
× Leverage (total assets/equity) . . .	2.24	2.10	2.52	2.34	2.16
= A/T ret on equity . . .	14.7%	20.0%	12.9%	24.7%	13.7%
× Earnings retention (1−dividend Pay Out)	0.58	0.65	0.35	0.59	0.51
= Internal growth of common equity	8.5%	13.0%	4.5%	14.5%	6.9%

Source: *Standard & Poor's Compustat Services, Inc.*, "Financial Dynamics Annual Financial Analysis and Standard & Poor's 400 Industrial Composite," 1982.

A second method available from Standard & Poor's Financial Dynamics Service is introduced to show the differences between companies' internal growth rates and return on stockholders' equity and to demonstrate many of the points made in this chapter.

Remembering that the two key points for the investor are stockholder's equity and return on stockholders' equity, you can note that the figures presented in Table 8-11 show some significant differences between companies. R. J. Reynolds' return on stockholders' equity is 20%, while American Telephone & Telegraph's is 12.9%. The internal growth rate of stockholders' equity is 13% for R. J. Reynolds, while American Telephone & Telegraph's is 4.5%. Total return for R. J. Reynolds is 19.0% (13% growth plus 6.0% yield) while American Telephone & Telegraph's is 13.1% (4.5% plus 8.6% yield). If "real earnings" were considered and underdepreciation accounted for, R. J. Reynolds would have to adjust its pre-tax income downward by 15%, while American Telephone & Telegraph would have to adjust its pre-tax income downward by 42%. This widens the difference between these two companies.

The investor in American Telephone & Telegraph would be better served by buying the bond of the company with a 11.38% yield to maturity and then compounding that income at 11.38% than he would be by buying the stock and receiving and 8.6% dividend yield plus an illusory growth in shareholders' equity of 4%. In real terms, American Telephone & Telegraph is actually liquidating its stockholders' equity per share.

On the other hand, the stockholders' equity for an investor in R. J. Reynolds is growing by 13.0%, while the investor is receiving a real dividend of 6% for a total return of 19%. Adjustment for underdepreciation would lower the total return form 19.0% to about 17.0%. Thus, the investor would be better served by buying R. J. Reynolds stock with a 17.0% compound return than by buying either the R. J. Reynolds bonds, which yield 11.43%, or government bonds that yield 11.25 to 11.50%. (Further discussion of these two companies' characteristics is presented in a later section on company examples.)

It is important for the investor to understand that the return on stockholders' equity is approximately 13%, ranging from 11% to 14%, for all American corporations. And this, in essence, is the same as a 13% coupon bond. Both earn 13% if purchased at book value for the stock, or at par value in the case of the bond. Once this relationship is established, the investor has a means of determining relative values and for beginning to determine which investment is really best for him, stocks or bonds.

This is why it is so important for the investor to be able to distinquish the "real earners" from the general population of possible common stock investments. Once the adjustments have been made to the return on equity figures and a "real earner" is uncovered, legitimate comparisons can be made between the total growth of "real earners," and the growth contingent upon collecting and reinvesting income from a bond.

Look for companies that can maintain an economic advantage. In a highly competitive economic environment, charged with political and social forces, it is difficult for a company or an industry consistently to earn an above-average return on stockholders' equity. With the subtle deterioration of shareholder wealth through inflation, it is even harder to find those companies that earn a true above-average return on shareholder equity.

Table 8-12. Industry characteristics with examples.

	Advantages	Examples
Monopoly or oligopoly market structure	Ability to raise prices and maintain barriers of entry to new competitors	Tobacco—R. J. Reynolds Ind. Broadcasting—Capital Cities Publishing— Washington Post Co.
Business franchise or strong product indentification	Ability to raise prices, retain loyal customers, and discourage competition	Specialized Financial Services— American Express Co.; GEICO Corp. Food companies— Nabisco Brands; Dart & Kraft Co.; Brown Foreman Distillers Corp.
Specialized services or products	Ability to raise prices, in a market not large enough to attract competitiors	Strum Ruger & Co.; Service Master, Inc.; Henredon Furniture, Inc.; Hillenbrand Industries
Commodity products no overcapacity	Low-cost producer has the only advantage: Most times the marginal producer determines the price structure	Dow Chemical Corp.
Overcapacity	No advantage	Old trunk airlines

Source: Bowen and Ganucheau.

The investor must seek and purchase stocks of companies that can maintain an economic advantage, leading to their maintaining above-average, although possibly fluctuating, rates of return on stockholders' equity. In addition, the investor must purchase these stocks at a low P/E ratio that, by mathematical definition, results in a price close to book value per share.

Four major categories into which different industries fall with their advantages and examples, are outlined in Table 8-12.

In summary, the information presented in this chapter provides several characteristics for the selection of good companies at reasonable prices.

First, select stocks with low P/E ratios as measured against bonds and other stocks. By definition, these stocks will sell at a price close to book value, depending on their payout ratios and their reinvestment opportunities.

Second, avoid high-unit-growth companies if the growth attracts competition, which would turn an economic exploitation into a commodity business. This can bring on price competition and its resulting pressures on profit margins. Also, high-unit growth probably would result in costly financing of capital spending to accommodate the growth.

Third, buy companies that have "real earnings," even in inflationary times, and that generate net free cash from operations. These companies are self-financing and can afford to finance their own growth.

Fourth, select a company that has an economic advantage in the product or service it provides. Table 8-12 is helpful in describing these advantages. A company with an economic advantage will have the freedom to raise prices and will be able to maintain the above-average returns on its invested capital.

Fifth, wait until the ideal investment becomes available. If stocks of companies having these characteristics are not currently available, invest in high-quality bonds maturing in three to five years until the next time these stocks become available at bargain prices. Successful investing depends not only on selecting companies and stocks with above-average potential but also on preserving capital when these high-quality investments are not available at the right price.

References

1. David F. Hawkins, "Inflation, Market Efficiency and Accounting Data: Keys to Identifying the Corporate and Investor Winners," *Accounting Bulletin 3, Drexel Burnham & Company,* May 1974, p. 13.
2. Richard Greene, "Are more Chryslers in the Offing?" *Forbes,* February 2, 1981, pp. 69-73.
3. Leopold A. Bernstein, *Financial Statement Analysis: Theory Application and Interpretation.* The Willard J. Graham Series in Accounting. Consulting ed. Robert N. Anthony. (Homewood, Ill.: Richard D. Irwin, 1978), pp. 360-371.
4. James A. Largay, III and Clyde P. Stickney, "Cash Flows, Ratio Analysis and the W. T. Grant Company Bankruptcy." *Financial Analysts Journal,* July-August 1980, pp. 184-187.
5. Barre W. Littel and Robert Levine, "Financial Quality Profile—Introduction to FQP Theory, Ratios and Scoring," *Kidder, Peabody & Company,* December 19, 1980, p. 3.
6. Michael E. Porter, "Industry Structure Competitive Strategy: Keys to Profitability," *Financial Analysts Journal,* July-August 1980, pp. 39-40.
7. Hawkins, "Inflation, Market Efficiency and Accounting Data," p. 20.
8. Peter F. Drucker, "Measuring Business Performance," *Wall Street Journal,* Editorial Page, August 3, 1976.
9. Arnold Bernhard, "Investing in Common Stocks," *Value Line Investment Survey,* 1975, p. 50.
10. *Standard & Poor's Compustat Services, Inc.,* Financial Dynamics Industrials, "Annual Financial Analysis," 1982.
11. Drucker, "Measuring Business Performance."
12. Ira Hersch, Theo N. Otis and William P. O'Commer, Jr., "Quality Measurement of Stock," *The Fourteen Research Corporation,* 1982, p. 17.
13. Barre W. Littel, "Excess Cash Flow Analysis—A New Approach to Determining Real Earnings, Dividend Sustainability, and Longer Term Growth of Corporations in an Era of Inflation," Kidder, Peabody & Company, May 6, 1975.

From Theory
to
Application

The previous chapter presented the most sophisticated version of the low P/E-ratio investment philosophy. Although this philosophy can be the most rewarding, it is not easy to apply. The investor is required to identify companies that can earn true profits and can maintain above-average rates of return on invested capital. This chapter provides more information for the investor to use in locating such companies.

Chapter 9 consists of four sections.

1. *How to analyze a company* gives a format that the investor can follow to better understand the value he is receiving for his invested dollar.

2. *Case study:* A discussion of International Harvester Company points out the weaknesses that have led to the company's current problems and how they would have been detected by the investor long before they became apparent.

3. *Case study:* The section on American Telephone & Telegraph Company covers a widely held stock, considered a sound investment. We will present this company, however, through the eyes of the true investor, giving a conclusion that differs from the consensus.

4. *Case study:* R. J. Reynolds Industries would be attractive to the investor even after the market averages have advanced 50% from the 1982 market lows.

After going through these four parts, you should be able to locate companies that have the characteristics of a good company, as described in chapter 8. By acquiring stocks of such companies when the price is right, the investor will own a portfolio of good companies, and will see his investment grow as the companies prosper.

How to analyze a company

To better understand what value the investor is receiving for his money, what economic advantages a company may have, and what returns on invested capital the company generates, the investor should make a thorough analysis of a company before he invests. To facilitate this analysis, he should gather the following items:

First, the company's annual reports for the latest three years.

Second, the most current Value Line Investment Survey, Ratings and Report on the company.

Third, the latest Standard & Poor's Compustat Services, Inc. Financial Dynamics, Annual Financial Analysis Sheet.

With this information, the investor can determine whether the company is worthy of investment, with the final determinant being the price.

A FORMAT FOR ANALYZING A COMPANY

The historical financial record

Stock information: Price: _____ Book value: _____
Ratio of price to book value: _____
Dividend yield: _____ P/E ratio: _____
No. of shares outstanding: _____
Normalized earnings yield: _____

Historical information: (**Year**)

	Average over the past five years		Average over the past ten years	
	Company	Value Line Industrial Composite	Company	Value Line Industrial Composite
Growth rates per share:				
Earnings per share growth	_____	_____	_____	_____
Dividend growth	_____	_____	_____	_____
Book value growth	_____	_____	_____	_____
Number of shares growth	_____	_____	_____	_____

Note: The investor should determine whether the book value has increased while the number of shares has decreased, has increased or has remained the same. Companies that require substantial reinvestment on the part of its shareholders should be avoided. The following information sheet can be completed using the company's annual report; the Value Line Service, i.e., VL; or Financial Dynamics Service; i.e., FD.

	Cumulative for the past five years		Cumulative for the past ten years	
Simplified free cash flow:	Company	Value Line Industrial Composite	Company	Value Line Industrial Composite
Cash flow per share	_____	_____	_____	_____
Less dividend per share	_____	_____	_____	_____
Less capital spending per share	_____	_____	_____	_____
Equals free cash flow per share	_____	_____	_____	_____
Negative free cash as a percent of cash flow	_____	_____	_____	_____

Free cash flow adjusted for depreciation:

	Current Year	Three Years
Cash flow per share	_____	_____
Less dividend per share	_____	_____
Less capital spending per share	_____	_____
Less current cost depreciation differential per share*	_____	_____
Equals free cash flow per share	_____	_____
Negative free cash as a percent of cash flow	_____	_____

Comparative ratios:

	Current Year		Average For the Past Three Years		Average For the Past Five Years	
	Company	VL/SP	Company	VL/SP	Company	VL/SP
(a) Liquidity ratios:						
Current ratio (FD)	_____	_____	_____	_____	_____	_____
Ratio of cash to current assets (FD)	_____	_____	_____	_____	_____	_____
Ratio of cash to current liabilities (FD)	_____	_____	_____	_____	_____	_____
(b) Margins:						
Operating margins (VL)	_____	_____	_____	_____	_____	_____
Net profit margins (VL)	_____	_____	_____	_____	_____	_____
(c) Capitalization ratios:						
Ratio of debt to equity (VL)	_____	_____	_____	_____	_____	_____
Ratio of equity to total invested capital (FD)	_____	_____	_____	_____	_____	_____
(d) After-tax return on investment:						
Return on equity (VL)	_____	_____	_____	_____	_____	_____
Return on total capital (VL)	_____	_____	_____	_____	_____	_____
Return on average total assets (FD)	_____	_____	_____	_____	_____	_____

(e) Plowback ratios:
   Ratio of retained
     earnings to common
     equity (VL) ____ ____ ____ ____ ____ ____
   Internal growth rate
     of common equity
     (FD) ____ ____ ____ ____ ____ ____
   Cash plowback ratio
     (14R) ____ ____ ____ ____ ____ ____
   Unit growth rate
     fundable (KP) ____ ____ ____ ____ ____ ____

(f) Other useful ratios:
   Asset turnover ratio
     (FD) ____ ____ ____ ____ ____ ____
   Tax ratio (VL) ____ ____ ____ ____ ____ ____
   Fixed charge coverage
     ratio (FD) ____ ____ ____ ____ ____ ____
   Dividend payout ratio
     (VL) ____ ____ ____ ____ ____ ____

VL = Value Line 900 Industrial Composite or Value Line Company sheets
SP = Standard & Poor's 400 Industrial Composite
FD = Financial Dynamics Annual Financial Analysis Company Review
14R = 14 Research Corporation Method
KP = Kidder-Peabody, Barre W. Littel's method

Comments:

Understated Asset Values:

* *Less current cost depreciation differential per share:*
To derive this figure, turn to the section in the annual report labeled "Inflation Accounting Data" or "Supplementary Data—Accounting for the Effects of Inflation (Unaudited)." In this section is found a table called Supplementary Financial Data or Consolidated Statement of Earnings Adjusted for the Effects of Changing Prices (Unaudited). There are three different numbers—historical cost, general inflation (constant dollar), and specific prices (current cost). The goal is to compare historical cost depreciation to current cost dollar depreciation. (Constant dollar depreciation will be close to current cost.) Subtract historical cost depreciation

from current cost depreciation and divide by the number of shares outstanding. Plug in the figure and note the change in the numbers. Most of the time it will be worse but how much worse is the important relationship.

Once this information is obtained, a company can be compared to other companies, or to the Value Line Industrial Composite of 900 companies, or to the Standard & Poor's Industrial Composite of 400 companies. The investor will then have the figures required to determine whether the company under consideration for purchase shows average or above-average performance.

Characteristics of the industry to which the company belongs can be studied by reading the Value Line Industry briefs located in the front of each industry section of the Value Line Investment Survey.

For more detailed information, a large library should give access to the Standard & Poor's Industry Surveys. These give detailed, fundamental information on different industries. Each industry is reported on in detail annually with an updated report each quarter. Also, some brokerage firms provide industry studies with useful information.

The key item to extract from these reports is a grasp of the economics of the industry being studied. Any forecasts should be taken with a grain of salt. The investor should concentrate on determining the importance of the company's products and the nature of competition in the industry. Also, he should be learning whether the company has any defined economic advantage and pricing power. Once this information has been discovered, the investor has a good idea of the quality of the company being studied. If the company has most of the "good characteristics," price then becomes the determining factor for investment.

As developed in chapters 3 and 6, the "Investor's Equation" will provide the answer to whether the price is attractive. You should recall that the "Investor's Equation" takes the earnings yield of the stock and converts it to an annuity payment. This annuity grows over time, that is, compounds, by the total return (current yield plus reinvestment rate) of the stock until it reaches $1.00.

The number of years it took to reach $1.00 is the time it took for the investment to double. This time period is then converted to a yield-to-maturity equivalent for a bond. This is done by calculating what interest rate or yield is necessary to double money in that same time period. This interest rate is then compared to the yield available on government bonds maturing in 10 to 20 years. If the return on the stock is higher than prevailing bond yields, that stock becomes the investment of choice. This calculation provides a method for determining whether the price of a stock is attractive.

If a business calculator or a compound interest table are not available, the investor may select stocks whose earnings yields are higher than the available yield on long-term government bonds, and which have an above-average, sustainable return-on-equity.

INTERNATIONAL HARVESTER COMPANY
A cash user with low profitability

International Harvester Company[1] is the largest manufacturer of heavy-duty and medium-duty trucks including school buses. The company is the second largest manufacturer of agricultural equipment in the United States offering a full line of farm equipment. International Harvester Company also has a small construction equipment division. The trade names used by International Harvester Company are McCormick, Cadet, Paystar, Loadstar, and Travstar. Seventy percent of International Harvester Company's sales are in the domestic market, while 30% are in the foreign market. International Harvester Company was founded 153 years ago by Cyrus H. McCormick, the man who perfected the reaper. This reaper improved the farmers' productivity and helped to launch the world's first industrial revolution.

The historical financial record

The tables that follow present International Harvester Company's financial profile over the past ten years.[2,3]

Stock information:

Price: $9.25	Book value: $-24.92
Ratio of price to book value: N/A	
Dividend Yield: 0	P/E ratio: N/A
No. of shares outstanding: 32,300,000	
Normalized earnings yield: N/A	

Historical information: 1982 *†

	Average over the Past Five Years		Average over the Past Ten Years	
Growth rates per share	International Harvester Company	Value Line Industrial Composite	International Harvester Company	Value Line Industrial Composite
Earnings per share growth	Deficit	9.0%	Deficit	10.5%
Dividend growth . .	− 12.0%	11.0%	− 5.0%	9.0%
Book value growth	− 16.0%	9.5%	− 6.0%	9.0%
Number of shares growth	2.1%	1.7%	1.7%	1.4%

	Cumulative for the Past Five Years		Cumulative for the Past Ten Years	
Simplified free cash flow	International Harvester Company	Value Line Industrial Composite	International Harvester Company	Value Line Industrial Composite
Cash flow per share	− $38.00	$28.88	$ 0.14	$46.49
Less dividend per share	− $ 7.25	$ 6.54	− $15.60	$10.48
Less capital spending per share	− $41.76	$28.12	− $69.87	$42.73
Equals free cash flow per share . .	− $87.01	− $ 5.78	− $85.33	− $ 6.72
Negative free cash as a percent of cash flow	NA	20.0%	NA	14.0%

Free cash flow adjusted for depreciation:	Current Year	Cumulative for the Past Three Years
Cash flow per share	− $46.78	− $ 63.74
Less dividend per share	0	− $ 2.80
Less capital spending per share	− $ 3.35	− $ 25.48
Less current cost depreciation differential per share.	− $ 2.80	− $ 8.12
Equals free cash flow per share	− $52.93	− $100.14
Negative free cash as a percent of cash flow	NA	NA

Comparative ratios:	Current Year		Average For the Past Three Years		Average For the Past Five Years	
	Int. Harv.	VL/SP	Int. Harv.	VL/SP	Int. Harv.	VL/SP
(a) Liquidity ratios:						
Current ratio (FD)......	1.5	1.5	1.5	1.5	1.6	1.6
Ratio of cash to current assets (FD)....	0.16	0.15	0.12	0.15	0.07	0.15
Ratio of cash to current liabilities (FD) .	0.23	0.22	0.17	0.22	0.11	0.22
(b) Margins:						
Operating margins (VL) .	NMF	11.4%	NMF	12.0%	NMF	12.6%
Net profit margins (VL) .	NMF	3.3%	NMF	4.2%	NMF	4.6%
(c) Capitalization ratios:						
Ratio of debt to equity (VL)..............	NMF	0.43	1.56	0.41	0.96	0.40
Ratio of equity to total invested capital (FD) ..	(−18)	0.61	23%	0.63	32.9%	0.64
(d) After-tax return on investment:						
Return on equity (VL) ..	NMF	9.6%	NMF	12.7%	NMF	13.8%
Return on total capital (VL)	NMF	8.3%	NMF	10.4%	NMF	11.2%
Return on average total assets (FD)	NMF	4.9%	NMF	6.2%	NMF	6.7%
(e) Plowback ratios:						
Ratio of retained earnings to common equity (VL)	NMF	4.4%	NMF	7.5%	NMF	8.6%
Internal growth rate of common equity (FD) ..	NMF	5.0%	NMF	7.6%	NMF	8.5%
Cash plowback ratio (14R)	NMF		NMF		NMF	
Unit growth rate fundable (KP)	NMF		NMF		NMF	

(f) Other useful ratios:

Asset turnover ratio (FD) .	0.95	1.22	1.12	1.32	1.35	1.34
Tax ratio (VL)	NMF	44.6%	NMF	44.4%	NMF	45.3%
Fixed charge coverage ratio (FD)	NMF	3.8x	NMF	4.8x	NMF	5.7x
Dividend payout ratio (VL)	100%	55.0%	107%	46.0%	93.0%	43.0%

NMF = Not a meaningful figure because of huge deficits.
 VL = Value Line 900 Industrial Composite or Value Line Company sheets.
 SP = Standard & Poor's 400 Industrial Composite.
 FD = Financial Dynamics Annual Financial Analysis Company Review.
 14R = 14 Research Corporation Method.
 KP = Kidder-Peabody, Barre W. Littel's method.

* Value Line Inc., Selections and Opinions, Value Line 900 Industrial Composite, July 1983.
† Standard & Poor's *Financial Dynamics Standard & Poor's 400 Industry Composite,* October 1983.

The financial ratios and statistics are not very meaningful because of the large deficits the company has incurred. By focusing, however, on a particular time period—1973 through 1977—and by presenting ratios from that period, an analyst can begin to see the results of poor financial management that led to International Harvester's problems in the late 1970s and early 1980s.

	International Harvester Company 1973-77	Value Line or S&P 400 Industrial Composite 1973-77
Margins:		
Operating margins (VL)	8.2%	13.6%
Net profit margins (VL).	2.6%	4.8%
After-tax return on investment:		
Return on equity (VL)	8.9%	13.2%
Return on total capital (VL) .	7.1%	10.5%
Return on average total assets (FD)	4.3%*	7.0%*
Plowback ratio:		
Ratio of retained earnings to common equity (VL) . . .	5.7%	8.4%
Internal growth rate of common equity (FD)	6.6%*	8.4%*

Simplified free cash flow:

Cash flow per share	$38.14	$17.61
Less dividend per share	– $ 8.35	– $ 3.94
Less capital spending per share	– $28.11	– $14.61
Equals free cash flow per share	$ 1.68	– $ 0.94
Negative free cash flow as a percent of cash flow	NA	5.3%

Growth rates:

Earnings per share growth . . .	15.7%	7.9%
Dividend growth	5.4%	10.1%
Book value growth	5.7%	8.6%
Number of shares growth . . .	1.2%	1.1%

* Standard & Poor's Compustat Services Inc., Financial Dynamics Annual Reports.

During the mid-'70s, International Harvester Company began its decline that would take it into the 1980s as a corporation fighting for its existence. By reviewing the financial statistics for the 1973-77 period, one can see that International Harvester's operating margins were 40% below the Value Line Industrial Composite's operating margins. Net profit margins were 46% below those of the Value Line Industrial Composites, and this led to a return on invested capital that was approximately 35% below the Value Line Industrial Composite's return on invested capital.

The "simplified free cash flow" figures for the period 1973 through 1977 show International Harvester was barely holding its own. However, with a more in-depth analysis of the statement listing the sources and uses of funds, the analyst obtains a different picture.

	Cumulative for 1973-1977
Cash flow and deferred taxes and earnings in uncol. subs . .	$ 1040.6
Less dividends	– 246.5
Less capital spending	– 792.6
Equals	1.5
Less other capital needs	– 282.5
Equals	– 281.0
Less maturing long-term debt . .	– 245.4
Equals free cash	– 526.4

"Other capital needs" reduces the picture to one of tremendous cash usage. International Harvester Company became a net user of $281 million through this five-year period. To make up this short-fall, the company borrowed more heavily. Long-term debt went from $497 million, or 28% of total invested capital, to $926 million, or 34% of total invested capital. Short-term debt was reduced from $519 million to $249 million, resulting in a decline of $270 million. The net result was to increase total debt by $159 million.

This deterioration of the balance sheet occurred during a time when International Harvester Company was in a cyclical rebound induced by the economy. Larger infusions of new cash were needed to keep the company rolling, in spite of the fact that the company was reporting record high earnings.

International Harvester's earnings increased from $3.86 to $6.92 a share. Cash flow rose from $6.64 to $10.04 a share. Operating margins rose from 7.5% to 9.1%, and the net profit margin rose from 2.6% to 3.4%. Sales rose from $4.19 billion to $5.97 billion. In spite of this cyclical rebound, profitability was still about 30% below the Value Line Industrial Composite's profitability. This, in turn, caused cash flow to fall constantly short of the company's needs for financing sales growth.

Sales growth becomes a negative

International Harvester Company was not earning enough money on sales or on invested capital to finance future growth of sales. In spite of the cyclical upturn and the inability to raise the prices of products or to reduce the cost of materials or labor to achieve average levels of profitability, below-average levels of profitability caused International Harvester to require more and more outside financing as sales rose. Sales growth became a negative factor for International Harvester.

In addition to these problems, International Harvester was also facing two competitors: Deere & Company and Caterpillar Tractor Company. Both were financially stronger. Just to remain competitive with Deere and Caterpillar, International Harvester estimated that it would need to spend nearly $700 million on new plants and equipment.

With pricing and profitability inadequate during relatively good times, what would happen in an economic slump when International Harvester's markets weakened?

This weakening of the market is exactly what happened during the following five years. International Harvester had two more satisfactory years, 1978 and 1979, with rising earnings and sales and debt increasing from $1,175.0 million to $1,359.0 million. Instead of using these years to reduce its debt, International Harvester raised its dividend and increased capital spending substantially. From this point, any downward turn in its markets would cause disaster.

The markets for International Harvester's products were in decent condition during the first half of 1980. A new management recognized that International Harvester's costs, especially for labor, were out of line with the industry. The labor union contracts were up for renewal, and International Harvester's management tried to reduce its labor cost to be in line with its competition.

A conflict ensued with both sides standing firm, not easing up on their demands. This resulted in a six-month strike, which cost International Harvester Company approximately $800 million.

International Harvester finally relented, and the labor force went back to work. But by then International Harvester's markets had softened considerably. The death blow had been struck. The company had a negative cash flow, its total debt went from $1,359.0 million to a peak of $2,427.0 million. Its long-term debt increased from 28% of its total capital to 57% of its total capital by the end of 1981. The following year, International Harvester had a negative net worth and, for all practical purposes, was bankrupt. International Harvester Company's net worth reached its highest point in 1979 at $2.2 billion. The company now has a net worth of minus $100 million.

Conclusion

International Harvester Company is a company that the wealth-accumulating investor would have avoided long before its problems surfaced. Although its products are of high quality, several firms compete in the same markets. The result was that International Harvester lacked the freedom and flexibility to raise the prices of its products as its costs rose.

This type of situation will erode profit margins, or keep them under pressure, especially to a company that does not have the lowest costs of production in its industry.

In addition to the lack of pricing power, International Harvester was a net user of cash, which required extensive external financing. The financing used most frequently was debt, which resulted in weakening the balance sheet. A company in a cyclical industry cannot afford to have a weak balance sheet, or the financial leverage will add to the impact of the business cycle on the financial health of the company. These characteristics, coupled with the low returns on invested capital and the lack of any economic advantage, should have signaled potential trouble years ago to any analyst following the company.

AMERICAN TELEPHONE & TELEGRAPH: A CASH USER

The company

American Telephone & Telegraph Company[4] and its subsidiaries provide telephone and related services throughout the United States. There are 20 locally operating telephone companies, wholly owned by American Telephone & Telegraph Company, and three telephone companies, partly owned by American Telephone & Telegraph.

Interstate long-distance networks interconnect American Telephone & Telegraph Company and independent telephone company lines and provide connecting links between the United States and telecommunications systems overseas.

Western Electric Company, a wholly owned subsidiary, manufactures and purchases telecommunication products and supplies for the American Telephone & Telegraph system. American Telephone & Telegraph also owns Bell Laboratories, which provides research and development services. American Telephone & Telegraph serves 85 million access lines, of which about 44 million are capable of direct-dialing overseas. American Telephone & Telegraph transmits some 550 million telephone calls a day.

The American Telephone & Telegraph system is considered to be the best in the world, an absolute marvel in customer service and convenience.

The historical financial record[5,6]

Stock information:
Price: $62		Book value: $69	
Ratio of price to book value: 0.90x			
Dividend yield: 8.7%		P/E ratio: 7.6x	
No. of shares outstanding: 896 million			
Normalized earnings yield: 13.2%			

Historical information: 1982*†

	Average over the Past Five Years		Average over the Past Ten Years	
Growth rates per share	AT&T	Value Line Industrial Composite	AT&T	Value Line Industrial Composite
Earnings per share growth	6.5%	9.0%	7.5%	10.5%
Dividend growth . .	6.5%	11.0%	7.0%	9.0%
Book value growth	4.0%	9.5%	4.0%	9.0%
Number of shares growth	6.7%	1.7%	4.9%	1.4%

	Cumulative for the Past Five Years		Cumulative for the Past Ten Years	
Simplified free cash flow	AT&T	Value Line Industrial Composite	AT&T	Value Line Industrial Composite
Cash flow per share	$85.05	$28.88	$147.71	$46.49
Less dividend per share	25.40	6.54	42.91	10.48
Less capital spending per share	105.77	28.12	189.22	42.73
Equals free cash flow per share . .	– $46.12	– $ 5.78	– $84.42	– $ 6.72
Negative free cash as a percent of cash flow	54.0%	20.0%	57.0%	14.0%

Free cash flow adjusted for depreciation:	Current Year	Cumulative for the Past Three Years
Cash flow per share	$17.39	$52.53
Less dividend per share	5.40	15.80
Less capital spending per share	18.74	63.50
Less current cost depreciation differential per share	6.56	18.19
Equals free cash flow per share	– $13.31	– $44.96
Negative free cash as a percent of cash flow	77.0%	86.0%

Comparative ratios:

	Current Year		Average For the Past Three Years		Average For the Past Five Years	
	AT&T	VL/SP	AT&T	VL/SP	AT&T	VL/SP
(a) Liquidity ratios:						
Current ratio (FD)......	0.90	1.5	0.7	1.5	0.7	1.6
Ratio of cash to current assets (FD)....	0.20	0.15	0.14	0.15	0.15	0.15
Ratio of cash to current liabilities (FD) .	0.18	0.22	0.11	0.22	0.10	0.22
(b) Margins:						
Operating margins (VL) .	36.8%	11.4%	38.0%	12.0%	38.8%	12.6%
Net profit margins (VL) .	10.7%	3.3%	11.5%	4.2%	12.0%	4.6%
(c) Capitalization ratios:						
Ratio of debt to equity (VL)...............	0.71	0.43	0.75	0.41	0.79	0.40
Ratio of equity to total invested capital (FD) ..	0.46	0.61	0.45	0.63	0.45	0.64
(d) After-tax return on investment:						
Return on equity (VL) ..	11.1%	9.6%	11.8%	12.7%	12.1%	13.8%
Return on total capital (VL)	8.2%	8.3%	8.3%	10.4%	8.3%	11.2%
Return on average total assets (FD)	4.9%	4.9%	5.1%	6.2%	5.1%	6.7%
(e) Plowback ratios:						
Ratio of retained earnings to common equity (VL)	3.6%	4.4%	4.3%	7.5%	4.5%	8.6%
Internal growth rate of common equity (FD) ..	3.4%	5.0%	4.2%	7.6%	4.5%	8.5%
Cash plowback ratio (14R)	7.4%		7.5%		7.4%	
Unit growth rate fundable (KP)	0.8%		1.4%		1.6%	

(f) Other useful ratios:

Asset turnover ratio (FD) .	0.46	1.22	0.44	1.32	0.43	1.34
Tax ratio (VL)	41.3%	44.6%	39.0%	44.4%	39.5%	45.3%
Fixed charge coverage ratio (FD)	3.8x	3.8x	3.5x	4.8x	3.7x	5.7x
Dividend payout ratio (VL)	71.0%	55.0%	66.7%	46.0%	64.8%	43.0%

VL = Value Line 900 Industrial Composite or Value Line Company sheets.
SP = Standard & Poor's 400 Industrial Composite.
FD = Financial Dynamics Annual Financial Analysis Company Review.
14R = 14 Research Corporation Method.
KP = Kidder-Peabody, Barre W. Littel's method.

* Value Line Inc., Selections and Opinions, Value Line 900 Industrial Composite, July 1983.
† Standard & Poor's *Financial Dynamics Standard & Poor's 400 Industry Composite*, October 1983.

A cash user

In spite of the fact that American Telephone & Telegraph provides the best telephone service in the world, its shareholders have fared poorly over the years. When earnings growth, dividends, and book value are compared with the Value Line 900 Company Industrial Composite, American Telephone & Telegraph performs poorly in all areas. As a monopoly, albeit regulated, American Telephone & Telegraph should earn at least average returns on employed capital and should finance growth without serious dilution of the value of the shareholders' ownership.

But the facts are that American Telephone & Telegraph is a cash user, constantly requiring new infusions of cash through dividend reinvestment, debt offerings, or new common stock offerings. American Telephone & Telegraph's growth in number of shares outstanding over the past five and ten years has been 6.7% and 4.9%, respectively, outstripping its growth in book value per share of 4.0% over the same period.

Absence of pricing power

What is lacking in the American Telephone & Telegraph financial picture is pricing power. The lack of that power in a highly capital-intensive industry leads to constant requirements for new cash, just to stay even. As a regulated monopoly, American Telephone & Telegraph should be guaranteed a competitive rate-of-return on equity. The actual achievement of the goal is difficult: This is because of timing lags between the time the rate relief was requested and received and actual current financial needs.

Since 1975, American Telephone & Telegraph's long-distance telephone rates have risen by 3.6% a year. Local telephone service has risen by 5.8% a year. During this same period, personal income rose by 10.6% a year, and the consumer price index rose by 8.6% a year.[7] Increases in the rates for telephone service have lagged behind average price increases by a wide margin. This is one of American Telephone & Telegraph's basic problems.

On the positive side, American Telephone & Telegraph has experienced good productivity increases. Sales-per-employee have risen by 10.9% per year over the past seven years. There has been improvement in the sales-per-dollar of average total assets, i.e., asset turnover, over the same period, from $0.38 to $0.46 of sales for every dollar of average total assets.

These factors would normally reduce the need for increases in the rates. It does not, however, because American Telephone & Telegraph is still very "capital intensive," capital intensive being a low sales volume compared to a large capital or plant-and-equipment base.

Average capital invested per employee went from $80,562 to $136,766 over the seven-year period, a growth of 7.9% per year.

As American Telephone & Telegraph struggles to increase productivity through more sales per employee and through more sales per dollar of average total assets, it, unfortunately, remains highly capital intensive. This capital intensity is a negative factor in the inflationary environment of the past few years, because the depreciation of the asset base is inadequate.

In the "simplified free cash-flow" calculations, American Telephone & Telegraph has a cash-flow shortfall equal to 54% of its cash flow, while the Value Line Industrials Composite has a cash-flow shortfall equal to 20% of its cash flow. In the cash flow adjusted for depreciation, American Telephone & Telegraph has a cash-flow shortfall equal to 86% of its cash flow. These figures show that, even if the dividend were completely eliminated, American Telephone & Telegraph would still have to obtain financing from external sources.

A circular problem

Through technological advances, American Telephone & Telegraph can replace old equipment with new equipment that is capable of a tremendous increase in workloads while lowering maintenance cost. This produces a significant increase in productivity. But the rate at which these advances are taking place is still very slow when compared to the systems' total assets. Current cost accounting adjusts depreciation for changes in specific prices.

On page 46 of its annual report for 1982, American Telephone & Telegraph states that these price changes for new plant facilities and equipment were less than the general increase in the rate of inflation because of the technological benefits and productivity improvements. This is the argument given to explain why telephone rates are rising more slowly than the Consumer Price Index. What is missing is the fact that American Telephone & Telegraph is depreciating its current plant and equipment at a substantially lower rate than it should be, resulting in higher reported profits and paying taxes on those profits that are not "real." American Telephone & Telegraph is paying dividends that, on a "real" earnings basis, have not been earned.

The proof of this circular problem is in American Telephone & Telegraph's financing requirements. Ten years ago, American Telephone & Telegraph had 554 million shares outstanding. Today the company has 896 million shares outstanding, and there have been no stock dividends or stock splits. The increase is all from necessary external financing. It seems that every time the stock sells at a price near its book value, American Telephone & Telegraph offers new stock, again diluting the value of the stock held by its shareholders.

The solution

The logical solution to American Telephone & Telegraph's problems is faster depreciation (this will result in lower reported earnings), higher prices for its telephone service, and much lower levels of inflation. Faster depreciation is already, in fact, being employed, and American Telephone & Telegraph estimates that, by 1985, it will have saved $3 billion a year in external financing. This is a significant amount. It offers a good beginning for solving some of the problems the company faces.

More must be done. Higher prices for telephone services are also seen in the future, when the system is divided into eight separate companies. While local telephone service charges will rise, long-distance telephone charges will probably drop, matching more competitive alternatives. The net effect should be a rise in cost of service.

However, with telephone service currently considered a "right" or "necessity," and with consumer groups beginning to pressure politicians and regulators concerning this issue, will the rate increases be large enough or timely enough to make any difference in the fundamentals already described? A lower level of inflation would help the fundamental situation dramatically, because this would reduce the problem of the depreciation of assets at too low a level and would reduce the cost of debt. This, in turn, would raise "real" earnings, lower the interest cost, and raise the return on total capital and the return on equity. Can the investor count on rates rising quickly enough and on inflation staying low enough to enable the company to earn a competitive "real" return on its capital?

Conclusion

Over the years, American Telephone & Telegraph's shareholders essentially have subsidized the telephone user by accepting a below-average rate of return on their investments, compared to average, alternative investments. For a tax-free investor, pension fund, or foundation, it would have been better to have invested in the intermediate-term bonds of American Telephone & Telegraph over the past ten years than to have invested in its stock. Given the present basic facts and company characteristics of American Telephone & Telegraph, it would seem an impossible task to change the company from a "cash user" to a "cash generator," or even to produce a significant reduction in cash usage. While it is possible that the "split-up" of American Telephone & Telegraph may give the individual companies a chance to change their financial situations for the better, should an investor commit money based on such a hope?

R. J. REYNOLDS INDUSTRIES: A CASH MACHINE

Many of the principles discussed in this book can be illustrated at the current time, early summer of 1983, by examining R. J. Reynolds Industries, Inc.[8] While the stock market has advanced by 50% since its August 1982 lows, and stocks now sell at ten times Wall Street's estimate of earnings for 1983, and corporate bond yields are moving up and yielding $11\frac{1}{2}\%$, R. J. Reynolds Industries' stock sells at 6.6 times the consensus estimate for 1983 and is up only 25% from its 1982 low of $40.

Obviously, the stock is cheap in relation to bonds and to stocks. But often there are good reasons for aberrations like these to exist. In the case of R. J. Reynolds Industries, however, we think Wall Street has missed the real value in this company, and that the stock presents an excellent buying opportunity at $48½ per share.

R. J. Reynolds Industries is a world-wide, consumer-goods company that markets its products and services in virtually every country in the world. What follows are brief descriptions of R. J. Reynolds Industries' subsidiary companies.

First, R. J. Reynolds Tobacco Company is the nation's largest manufacturer of cigarettes sold in the United States. The company manufactures more than 20 brands in four major product classifications: cigarettes, smoking tobacco, chewing tobacco, and small cigars.

Second, R. J. Reynolds Tobacco International directs R. J. Reynolds' tobacco operations outside the United States.

Third, Del Monte Corporation is a diversified, international foods company, the largest canner of fruits and vegetables in the United States.

Fourth, Heublein Spirits & Wine Company, an international marketer of quality brands of alcoholic beverages, is the second largest producer of distilled spirits and wines in the United States.

Fifth, Kentucky Fried Chicken Company is the world's largest fast-service restaurant system.

Sixth, Aminoil U.S.A. is the second-largest independent petroleum exploration and production company in the United States. The company is also engaged in international exploration and production.

Seventh, Sea-Land Industries is the parent company of the world's largest container shipping company.

Eighth, R. J. Reynolds Development Corporation is responsible for creating new growth for R. J. Reynolds Industries by establishing a presence in new or related businesses and by generating new, profitable growth from existing business units.

The percentages of contributions from the company's various lines of businesses to net sales and revenues and the earnings from operations during the past three years are as follows.

Net sales and revenues (in percent)	1982	1981	1980
Tobacco..............	50	52	54
Food and beverage	24	20	20
Transportation	12	14	14
Energy..............	10	11	9
Other businesses	4	3	3
	100	100	100

Earnings from operations (in percent)	1982	1981	1980
Tobacco	70	69	73
Food and beverage	6	7	7
Transportation	9	6	5
Energy..............	13	16	14
Other businesses	2	2	1
	100	100	100

The historical financial record[9, 10]

Stock information: Price: $48½   Book value: $42
Ratio of price to book value: 1.13
Dividend yield: 6.12%   P/E ratio: 6.0x
No. of shares outstanding: 112.6 MM
Normalized earnings yield: 16.6%

Historical information: 1982*†

	Average over the Past Five Years		Average over the Past Ten Years	
Growth rates per share	R. J. Reynolds	Value Line Industrial Composite	R. J. Reynolds	Value Line Industrial Composite
Earnings per share growth........	12.5%	9.0%	11.0%	10.5%
Dividend growth ..	10.0%	11.0%	7.5%	9.0%
Book value growth	12.5%	9.5%	13.5%	9.0%
Number of shares growth	3.2%	1.7%	3.0%	1.4%

Simplified free cash flow	Cumulative for the Past Five Years		Cumulative for the Past Ten Years	
	R. J. Reynolds	Value Line Industrial Composite	R. J. Reynolds	Value Line Industrial Composite
Cash flow per share	$47.27	$28.88	$73.33	$46.49
Less dividend per share	11.27	6.54	18.67	10.48
Less capital spending per share	34.08	28.12	46.73	42.73
Equals free cash flow per share . .	$ 1.92	– $ 5.78	$ 7.93	– $ 6.72
Negative free cash as a percent of cash flow	NA	20.0%	NA	14.0%

Free cash flow adjusted for depreciation:	Current Year	Cumulative for the Past Three Years
Cash flow per share	$11.76	$32.24
Less dividend per share	2.85	7.53
Less capital spending per share	7.36	23.37
Less current cost depreciation differential per share	2.10	6.15
Equals free cash flow per share	– $ 0.55	– $ 4.81
Negative free cash as a percent of cash flow	5.0%	15.0%

Comparative ratios:

	Current Year		Average For the Past Three Years		Average For the Past Five Years	
	R.J.R.	VL/SP	R.J.R.	VL/SP	R.J.R.	VL/SP
(a) Liquidity ratios:						
Current ratio (FD)	2.0	1.5	2.0	1.5	2.2	1.6
Ratio of cash to current assets (FD)	0.06	0.15	0.04	0.15	0.05	0.15
Ratio of cash to current liabilities (FD) .	0.12	0.22	0.09	0.22	0.10	0.22

(b) Margins:

Operating margins (VL)	15.9%	11.4%	16.0%	12.0%	15.9%	12.6%
Net profit margins (VL)	6.7%	3.3%	6.6%	4.2%	6.5%	4.6%

(c) Capitalization ratios:

Ratio of debt to equity (VL)	0.31	0.43	0.28	0.41	0.30	0.40
Ratio of equity to total invested capital (FD)	0.62	0.61	0.64	0.63	0.66	0.64

(d) After-tax return on investment:

Return on equity (VL)	16.1%	9.6%	17.3%	12.7%	17.0%	13.8%
Return on total capital (VL)	13.3%	8.3%	14.5%	10.4%	14.2%	11.2%
Return on average total assets (FD)	9.4%	4.9%	9.7%	6.2%	9.8%	6.7%

(e) Plowback ratios:

Ratio of retained earnings to common equity (VL)	11.1%	4.4%	11.8%	7.5%	11.4%	8.6%
Internal growth rate of common equity (FD)	11.8%	5.0%	12.5%	7.6%	11.9%	8.5%
Cash plowback ratio (14R)	12.4%		12.5%		12.5%	
Unit growth rate fundable (KP)	0.8%		6.5%		6.4%	

(f) Other useful ratios:

Asset turnover ratio (FD)	1.18x	1.22x	1.22x	1.32x	1.21x	1.34x
Tax ratio (VL)	46.0%	44.6%	44.1%	44.4%	45.3%	45.3%
Fixed charge coverage ratio (FD)	6.4x	3.8x	6.4x	4.8x	7.3x	5.7x
Dividend payout ratio (VL)	39.0%	55.0%	38.0%	46.0%	39.0%	43.0%

VL = Value Line 900 Industrial Composite or Value Line Company sheets.
SP = Standard & Poor's 400 Industrial Composite.
FD = Financial Dynamics Annual Financial Analysis Company Review.
14R = 14 Research Corporation Method.
KP = Kidder-Peabody, Barre W. Littel's method.

* Value Line, Inc., Selections and Opinions, Value Line 900 Industrial Composite, July 1983.
† Standard & Poor's Financial Dynamics, S & P's Industrial Composite, October 1983.

By far the most significant impact on sales and earnings for Reynolds is from the tobacco division. It is because of this significance that we think the company is misunderstood and is not recommended by most analysts. Yet it is the tobacco division that gives Reynolds its unique investment characteristic. First, the negative case will be discussed.

The tobacco industry is a mature industry and, as such, does not experience much, if any, unit growth of its products. Over the past several years, unit growth for the industry has been about 1% per year. This is a fact that Wall Street finds very unappealing for investment prospects. After all, common stocks are for growth. How can companies grow that do not see increasing demand for their products? Some analysts even suggest that unit growth may be flat or becoming negative, and that this would not be good for long-term investment.

Another factor Wall Street analysts are concerned about is the ability of the tobacco companies to raise the prices of their products. Although unit growth has been almost flat over the past several years, revenues have increased because prices of products have risen. Some contend that cigarette prices have risen in line with inflation, while others say that the rate is below the inflation rate. This difference of opinion can be caused by the time period in which prices and inflation are measured and by whether wholesale or retail prices are used. The point is that, over long periods of time, the rise in prices for tobacco products is generally in line with the rise in inflation. Some Wall Street analysts speculate that the ability of the tobacco companies to raise the prices of products may be very limited in the future. Hence they may experience no unit growth and, possibly, no price growth. Why, then, should anyone own stock in a tobacco company?

Many of the characteristics that appear to be negative are construed by us as being positive. It is true that the tobacco industry is mature, that there is little or no unit growth. There is very little probability that the market will be entered by competitors who might erode profit margins or reduce the return-on-assets of the tobacco division.

The gross margin on tobacco was 17.4% for 1982, and the pre-tax return-on-assets was 37.7%.

Another reason new entrants would be severely limited would be the ban on television advertising, which makes it difficult for a new company to begin marketing its products. In addition to the difficulty of advertising a new product, it would be difficult, in many cases, for a new company to obtain vending-machine and/or counter space for its products. All in all, these high returns are very well protected from new competition, not new brands, but new companies.

The tobacco industry is characterized by oligopoly pricing. Usually one company exercises price leadership, and the other companies follow suit. Other than coupons and other promotions, there is no real price competition in the industry. Lowering prices by 10% probably would not increase sales to existing customers or encourage people to begin smoking. Smokers are generally very loyal to a brand and tend to identify with the particular brand they smoke. Several years ago, one of the authors smoked and, when out of cigarettes, would make several stops, if needed, to purchase his particular brand. This loyalty to a brand creates a strong consumer franchise. R. J. Reynolds Industries has several of the leading brands—Winston, Camel, and Salem.

Another interesting characteristic of the cigarette business is that there are no reasonable substitutes for cigarettes. Although smokers will chew gum and eat candy if they try to stop smoking or cut back, these do not satisfy the urge to smoke. Sooner or later, many return to cigarettes or to some other tobacco product.

In summary, the reader will conclude that Reynolds Industries is a price leader in an ologopoly market and that its products have strong brand identification. The industry can advertise through any media except television. Since there is low unit growth, it would be difficult for a new company to establish its brands. As a result, the probability of new competition entering the market is slim. The tobacco industry is highly profitable. Its high profit margins are protected because of these characteristics. But how does the investor benefit from these positive economic characteristics?

On page 56 of R. J. Reynolds Industries' annual report for 1982, the investor will find a table showing funds provided by operations. The total of income from operations minus taxes plus non-cash charges such as depreciation is commonly referred to as "cash flow from operations." From the tobacco operation alone, the company generated $739 million of after-tax cash flow in 1982. By dividing this by the number of shares outstanding, 106,706,000, an analyst can calculate the cash flow per share from the tobacco operations. This is: 739 divided by 106.7 equals $6.92. If an investor purchases Reynolds Industries' stock at $48.50 per share, he purchases the stock at seven times the previous year's cash flow, or at a cash flow yield of 14¼%: one divided by seven equals .1425.

Another characteristic of the tobacco industry is that it does not require much reinvestment of earnings to keep the basic business viable. There are very few research and development costs. Product obsolescence is not a problem. Therefore, plant and equipment are not outdated. Most of their cash flow is not required for operating expenses. It can be directed into other assets.

It should be noted that depreciation for 1982, for Reynolds' tobacco division, was $75 million, and that capital expenditures were $226 million, or

$151 million in excess of depreciation, but substantially less than cash flow from the tobacco operation.

From previous discussions on the importance of wealth accumulation through the reinvestment of earnings, you will note that, assuming all the money is retained in the business, the book value (or asset value) of the business will grow by the $739 million of cash flow just from the tobacco division, less the $75 million of depreciation, or by $664 million.

R. J. Reynolds Industries has elected to invest $226 million in the tobacco segment, much of which will go for new machinery that will reduce production costs over the next several years. Since lower costs should enable Reynolds Industries to improve margins or to at least maintain existing margins, these reinvested earnings should generate high returns. The balance of the cash flow is available for dividends or can be reinvested in other divisions or in new businesses.

When an investor acquires an interest in Reynolds Industries at $48.50, he is purchasing an investment similar to a bond. The tobacco business alone provides a cash flow return of 14¼%. Because the company has the ability to raise prices of products and to pass along these costs, this cash flow is protected from the negative effects of inflation. From the period from 1978 through 1982, funds provided by tobacco operations increased at a 12.8% annualized compound rate, while the Consumer Price Index rose at a 10.31% annual compound rate. Not bad for a nongrowth business!

The gross margin on sales, earnings before taxes divided by sales, for tobacco products remained the same at 17% in 1978 as well as in 1982. This occurred because of the lack of new competition to drive down profit margins, and because of the company's ability to pass through cost increases.

We look at the tobacco business as being a "big cash machine" that continually pours cash out to its owners. At this time, there does not seem to be an end to its cascade of reinvestible cash. The big question the investor needs to answer is how the cash is being used and if the reinvested cash generates a competitive return.

The first benefit the investor receives is the dividend. Reynolds Industries' management has increased the dividend for 29 consecutive years, except for the federal government dividend freeze control year of 1971. The current dividend is $3, which provides a yield of 6.12% at a price of $48.50 per share. The probability of future increases in dividends is extremely high, as cash flows from operations should rise over time.

The cash retained in the business has been used to enter other businesses, as the previously mentioned corporate description would indicate. The returns from these other operating segments are not as high or as stable as the returns from the tobacco business. For the corporation as a whole, however, funds provided by operations have exceeded the sum of capital expenditures plus cash dividends paid during the past five years. This leaves about $860 million of internally generated funds available for other company purposes. This performance was achieved in spite of heavy capital investment in recent years in the company's capital-intensive energy and transportation businesses. The company expects internally generated funds to be sufficient to meet projected capital expenditures and cash dividends over the next three years. The investor is a part owner in a company that can and will expand without requiring additional investment by the investor. This type of growth is a key element in the accumulation of wealth.

Why not contact R. J. Reynolds Industries and obtain their latest annual report? Their accounting methods are understandable. Management provides adequate discussion about the various businesses as well as financial data. The company generates above-average returns on equity as well as on total capital. And, as mentioned earlier, it is a generator of net free cash. The balance sheet is conservative. The stock sells at a low P/E ratio with an above-average dividend yield. We are of the opinion that Wall Street is more interested in trying to explain why stock prices move and is less interested in understanding the accumulation of wealth by a business. We believe that Reynolds Industries is a neglected stock in a rising market.

Conclusion

After examining the case studies, you should have an understanding of the factors that make some companies attractive for long-term investment. These case studies apply most of the principles that build a workable philosophy. Proof that this philosophy works is demonstrated in the return that was obtainable from R. J. Reynolds Industries' stock over the past five years. Had an investor purchased stock in Reynolds Industries at its average price of $29.30 in 1978, and sold the stock at $54.38, its average price for 1983, he would have realized a five-year compound rate of return, including price appreciation and dividends, of 19% plus per year. As impressive as that return may be, the investor should bear in mind that the stock is still attractively priced, allowing him to continue to hold and to compound at an above-average rate. This current attractiveness is based on two very important items stressed in the philosophy: price and the economics of the business. The characteristics that made Reynolds Industries a wealth-accumulating company over the past five years are still intact today, and should remain so in the foreseeable future.

For those readers who would like to learn more about value investing, we have included a suggested reading list, Appendix B. Some of the listings are sources cited in this book and are included in the bibliography. The list also contains some material not included in the bibliography, but which influenced the development of the philosophy presented in this book.

References

1. International Harvester Company, Notice of Special Meeting of Stockholders, October 28, 1982.
2. Standard & Poor's Compustat Services, Inc., *Financial Dynamics Industrials*, "Annual Financial Analysis," March 24, 1982.
3. Value Line Incorporated, *Value Line Investment Survey*, "Ratings & Reports," August 28, 1983, p. 1437.
4. American Telephone & Telegraph Company, *Annual Report*, 1982, 1981, 1980.
5. Standard & Poor's Compustat Services, Inc., *Financial Dynamics Industrials*, "Annual Financial Analysis," April 20, 1983.
6. Value Line Incorporated, *Value Line Investment Survey*, "Ratings and Reports," July 29, 1983, p. 751.
7. Standard & Poor's Compustat Services, Inc., Standard & Poor's Industrial Survey, *Telecommunications Basic Analysis*, October 14, 1982, pp. 30-31.
8. R. J. Reynolds Industries, *Annual Report*, 1982, p. 56.
9. Standard & Poor's Compustat Service, Inc., *Financial Dynamics Industrials*, "Annual Financial Analysis," May 16, 1983.
10. Value Line Incorporated, *Value Line Investment Survey*, "Ratings and Reports," October 7, 1983, p. 335.

CHAPTER 10

How to
Implement a Low
P/E Ratio Philosophy

The last few chapters have dealt with the most sophisticated version of the low P/E-ratio philosophy, philosophy C. After reading these chapters, you should have the knowledge needed to identify good-quality companies for long-term investment purposes. The case study of R. J. Reynolds Industries demonstrates the value to the true investor of being able to find good companies at the right price. Simply buying this stock at its average high and low price in 1978 and selling it at its average high and low price in 1983 would have provided the investor with an excellent return. The ideal portfolio would be composed of 15 of these good companies, which would result in an extremely low portfolio turnover, greatly reducing taxes and commission costs.

Before you set out to find 15 or more companies that qualify under philosophy C, we must point out two items: First, there are not that many companies that meet philosophy-C requirements. Second, such stocks are not always available at the right price. As a result of free competition, the number of companies that can sustain above-average rates of return on invested capital is limited. As we mentioned earlier, competition acts to drive down the rate of return on invested capital to that which would be earned by the economists "perfectly competitive" industry.

Obviously, not many of the large capitalization-type companies will enjoy these privileged positions. Their size and obvious prosperity will tend to attract other competitors. The first rule, then, in looking for companies that are suitable for philosophy C is to look for those with smaller capitalization, those that have a product niche and are not as visible as the Sears and General Motors of the world.

By broadening your horizons and reading a lot of annual reports, you, as the true investor, can locate more than 15 philosophy-C companies, particularly if you are a professional investor or a very sophisticated amateur.

Once located, however, your problem is being able to buy these companies at the right price. In the past couple of years, with a bull market in progress, it has become increasingly difficult to find such companies at reasonable prices.

Currently, with bonds cheaper than the average stock, it is important to exercise patience and buy the right stock at the right price. If an investor pays too much for his position in even an excellent company, his results will probably turn out to be disappointing. For more information concerning the importance of paying the right price, take a look at the appendix titled "Price vs. the Reinvestment Rate."

For the true investor, the best market for locating good values is a severe bear market similar to the one of 1974. During these extreme price breaks, an investor would be able to easily find 15 or more philosophy-C companies at excellent prices. Also, the true investor recognizes that bear markets always end, and that, eventually, the market will reflect the values in businesses he owns.

While the bargains become available in bear markets, the investor prospers in bull markets. Often he must commit funds to new ventures, even when philosophy-C companies are not available. As mentioned earlier, when such is the case, the investor can purchase three- to five-year government bonds until bargains again appear. There may be cases, however, where an investor can't use bonds for either legal or personal reasons. How does this investor handle the situation?

When the investor is unable to obtain enough philosophy-C companies, we suggest supplementing the portfolio with philosophy-B companies. Almost always, there are low P/E-ratio stocks available that will meet the four or five filters the investor may choose. Obviously, where philosophy-C companies are available at the right price, they should be acquired for the portfolio. More than likely, the investor will have five to ten C companies and ten to fifteen B companies in his portfolio. It is wise to recognize the difference between companies of the R. J. Reynolds Industries type and philosophy B-type companies. The difference will indicate how these holdings are treated in the portfolio.

As mentioned in chapter 8, C companies need not be sold unless (a) the economics of the business change and the company no longer enjoys a position that will enable it to earn above-average returns on its invested capital; (b) the management begins to think more about perpetuating its empire than building shareholders' wealth; or (c) the price of the stock has risen to where it substantially overdiscounts the present value of the company and its future potential, enabling funds to be better deployed in another situation.

If an investor is sure he has located a philosophy-C company, not only is he immune from selling his holdings for several years, but, as prices fluctuate from year to year, he can add to to his holdings on price declines. Not only could the investor have purchased R. J. Reynolds Industries in 1978 and still have held it through 1983, he could have added to his holdings on price dips in any one of the five years. When a C company is found, as price permits, it can be a re-occurring acquisition, absorbing investable cash flows. This is not the case with philosophy-B companies.

Philosophy-B companies, (those offering low P/E-ratio stocks that meet several quality filters referred to as B companies), are purchased with the idea that they will later be sold. They don't have all the good characteristics of philosophy-C companies, characteristics that enable them to be held for long-term compounding purposes. Stocks meeting the requirements of philosophy B, however, are more available and less difficult to analyze. That is why this is the basic philosophy used in building a portfolio, and why the investor should label some companies "C" and others "B."

The ease of constructing a portfolio of B stocks can be shown by the model portfolio we put together at the beginning of 1982. We got a list of the Standard & Poor's 400 as of December 31, 1981, with the stocks ranked by their P/E ratio from low to high. We then decided on three criteria the stocks had to meet to be included in our portfolio:

1. The P/E ratio must be in the bottom 12½% of the Standard & Poor's 400.
2. The stocks must have a Standard & Poor's quality rating of A− or better.
3. The stock's dividend yield must be at least 40% of the current bond yield (15%).

The portfolio has an average P/E ratio of 5 and a dividend yield of 7.3%. Two banks that also met the criteria were added to the list of industrial companies for purposes of diversification, resulting in 22 companies and 14 industries being respresented (Table 10-1).

We assumed equal dollar amounts of the stocks were purchased, and held until the following December 31. No economic forecasting or timing were involved. The portfolio was 100% invested all year. Not only are the results for some of the individual stocks extremely interesting, but the entire portfolio returned 23% more than Standard & Poor's 500.

We believe any variables the investor chooses, in addition to the P/E ratio, should focus on how the company is financed and on shareholder equity growth. As we said earlier, examples of standards an investor may use in this approach are:

1. Low debt-to-equity ratio.
2. High dividend yield.

Table 10-1. Model portfolio.

Company	P/E Ratio	Price 12-31-81	Yield	Price 12-31-82	% Chg. '81-82
Texaco	3.8	33.00	9.1	31.125	− 5.7
Boeing	4.0	22.50	6.2	33.875	+ 50.6
Continental Group	4.2	22.50	6.2	34.375	+ 3.8
Mobil Corp.	4.3	24.12	8.3	25.125	+ 4.2
Exxon	4.4	31.25	9.6	29.75	− 4.8
Cone Mills	4.8	30.87	7.1	33.625	+ 8.9
Westinghouse Electric	5.0	25.50	7.1	38.875	+ 52.5
Mead Corp.	5.1	23.00	8.7	18.75	− 18.5
Aluminum Co. America	5.2	25.62	6.4	31.00	+ 21.0
American Stand.	5.3	29.75	7.4	30.00	+ 1.0
Union Carbide	5.3	51.37	6.6	52.875	+ 2.9
Scott Paper	5.4	16.00	6.2	20.25	+ 26.6
Xerox Corp.	5.4	40.50	7.4	37.375	− 7.7
Borden	5.4	28.00	7.3	47.625	+ 70.1
Bemis	5.5	24.37	6.6	33.50	+ 37.5
PPG Inds.	5.5	37.75	6.3	51.75	+ 37.1
J. C. Penney	5.6	28.62	6.4	48.375	+ 69.0
Gulf Oil	5.6	35.37	7.9	29.75	− 15.9
Armco, Inc.	5.7	28.00	5.4	16.375	− 41.5
West Point Pepperell	5.8	22.87	7.9	38.375	+ 67.7
Chemical Bank	4.3	54.50	7.0	60.81	+ 11.6
Manufacturers Hanover	4.9	35.625	8.2	41.625	+ 16.8
			7.3		+ 17.6

7.3 + 17.6 = 24.9% total return.

Standard & Poor's 500 for Year 1982 = 20.3% total return.

3. Strong current ratio.
4. No loss years in the past five years.
5. Earnings growth of at least 7% per year over the past five years.
6. A Standard & Poor's quality rating on the company's bonds of A or better.
7. An above-average return on equity over the past five years.
8. An above-average Standard & Poor's stock rating.

By applying a few of these standards, a portfolio of quality stocks can be acquired that should, over the long run, provide above-average returns.

The first step in locating B stocks is to get a list of stocks ranked by P/E ratios. Major Wall Street brokerage firms should be able to supply the investor with this information, particularly if they have a quantitative or statistical service department.

Any large universe of stocks will suffice, the larger the better. This will become a more statistically representative sampling, enabling you to define at that time what constitutes a low P/E ratio. Tests have shown that the lower the P/E ratio, the higher the expected results will be. So keep your parameter in the lowest 25% to 30%.

If your broker can't give you a list containing a universe large enough to select 20 stocks, there are some other sources you can use. The Value Line Service has, in its statistical section, a list of low P/E-ratio stocks. We suggest when using any screen that utilities and financial stocks be eliminated, since utilities are very capital-intensive and, on the average, are cash users.

Financial companies such as banks and insurers have unique accounting and economic characteristics, making them different from the average company for analysis and investments.

We almost always avoid utilities. As shown in our model portfolio, however, we will use financial stocks that meet certain quality criteria.

Another source of ideas is David Dreman's column, "The Contrarian," appearing in *Forbes* in alternate issues. Dreman writes generally on low P/E investing and always gives several timely picks.

The investor willing to spend a few hundred dollars to subscribe to a service providing a screening of low P/E-ratio stocks can receive the *Graham Rea Investment Analysis* on a monthly basis.

As discussed in *The Money Masters,* Ben Graham during his later years did research using separately two criteria for selecting stocks. The first was that a stock's earnings yield should be twice the prevailing AAA bond yield. Also, the debt owed by the company should be less than the worth of the company. The second criterion was that the dividend yield should be no less than two thirds of the AAA bond yield, and, again, the company's debt should be less than its worth.

From the tests Graham ran over a 50-year period, 1925–1975, using these two variables combined with balance sheet quality, he found that the selected stocks produced return consistently above 15% per annum, or over double the record of the Dow Jones Industrial Average.

Graham's rules for selling a stock were quite simple. First, sell after the stock has gone up 50% or after two years, whichever comes first. Second, sell if the dividend is omitted. Third, sell when earnings decline so far that the current market price is 50% more than the new target buying price (Train, *The Money Masters,* p. 105).

In Graham's later years, his research and investing were done with an associate, James Buchanan Rea. Rea's firm publishes a list of stocks that have been screened to meet these stringent P/E ratio and balance sheet requirements. For the investor who is not interested in selecting stocks and managing his own portfolio, Rea also manages a mutual fund applying these same principles. The fund is open to the public, and more information about it is included in Appendix B.

When screens or investment services are not available, the investor may have a hard time evaluating the P/E ratio of a stock. Without a universe that ranks stocks, it will also be difficult to determine how cheap is cheap. Also, if the internal growth rate is unknown or a business calculator and/or compound interest table are not available, the investor will be unable to calculate the Investor's Equation.

How then does an investor define cheap or determine if a stock is cheap enough for investment? We recommend that you use the "margin of safety" concept discussed by Ben Graham in his book, *The Intelligent Investor* (p. 279). The margin of safety is the excess of the stock's earnings yield over the prevailing bond yield. In other words, if the current yield on ten-year treasury bonds is 12%, the investor should seek companies whose earnings yield is 12% × 1.3, or 15.6%. The reciprocal of 15.6 becomes the P/E ratio that provides a margin of safety in the common stock investment: 1/15.6 = 6.4x. This approach is consistent with the other benchmarks we have defined, since it measures value relative to the income stream obtainable on bonds.

Once the investor has determined a benchmark for value, he can turn to various research sources for ideas. Brokerage reports can be useful if they describe current value, but should be avoided if they rely mostly on forecasts, particularly two years into the future. Again, we recommend the use of Value Line. For the investor willing to spend time looking for ideas, Value Line is an ideal source covering over 1,700 companies. Each week a new section of company reports is published, and the entire universe is reviewed or updated every 13 weeks. For each company there is enough statistical and historical information available to begin any analysis.

The material is presented in a well-organized, consistent manner. Within minutes, an investor can be familiar with a company's earnings yield, balance sheet quality, cash-flow characteristics, earnings history, and returns on invested capital. Armed with the Investor's Equation or the margin of safety concept, any investor willing to spend some time searching for ideas will find plenty in Value Line, and will have many of his filters answered in each company's write-up.

As mentioned earlier, we don't accept point-to-point earnings estimates. Again, we don't believe anyone can forecast the future. A problem in selecting individual holdings can be the cyclicality of some companies' earnings. A company may appear to be selling at a low P/E ratio because its earnings are at a cyclical peak and are about to decline. One way to avoid these companies is to look at the stability of a company's earnings over a period of five years.

We focus, not on precise year-to-year earnings, but rather on the past and potential returns on invested capital. Although the return on equity will fluctuate year to year, causing earnings-per-share fluctuations, we think estimating the normalized return on capital is much more reliable than short-term earnings estimates. From this normalized return-on-equity number, an investor can calculate a P/E ratio based on normalized earnings. To determine a normal return on equity he should examine the past several years' returns to see whether the business has changed, enabling it to earn more on its invested capital, or if analysts' earnings expectations are too optimistic. Often, analysts think current bonanzas will last indefinitely, and their estimates reflect their optimism.

Another excellent source of stock ideas—one that is free to most investors, compliments of their broker—is the Standard & Poor's *Stock Guide.* This compact book covers several thousand common stocks, giving such information as quality ratings, balance sheet data, earnings history, and P/E ratios. If you have a current issue and one from three years ago in searching out cheap stocks, you can have sufficient information to establish an earnings history for the company and how it has financed itself.

For example, you can determine if the number of shares has increased significantly. If you've located what appears to be an excellent buy, your next step is to get an annual report.

One of the best sources for investment information—and one that is free—is the business section of the public library. Not only is the Value Line Investment Survey available, but also publications from Standard & Poor's and Moody's Investors Service

Standard & Poor's "The Outlook" periodically carries screens of low P/E-ratio stocks as well as timely information. Standard & Poor's *Industry Survey* has current information about various industries and can supplement other research reports.

The Moody's manuals are extremely helpful in providing historical and statistical information on a large universe of companies, both industrial and financial.

Finally, the *Wall Street Journal* and *Barron's* have timely news and statistical information on earnings, P/E ratios, and yields. In short, for the serious investor wishing to develop his own ideas and have ample resources available, the public library is an excellent supplier of business data.

After you have assembled enough information to construct a portfolio, you need to know when to sell. This is perhapas more difficult than buying. Even many professional investors admit that one of their greatest weaknesses is determining when to sell. Often an investor makes an excellent purchase of a cheap stock, waits patiently for it to rise, and sees it advance 50% or more. Instead of selling into the price rise, he begins to believe the story that is pushing the stock's price higher and higher. No action is taken. A year later, the stock is out of favor. Most of the advance is lost. Again, an investor must not fall prey to the crowd's emotions if he wishes to succeed.

Philosophy-C companies need not be sold unless there are fundamental changes in the business, or their prices become too high relative to their real values.

On the other hand, philosophy-B companies are purchased because they are cheap, with the intention that they will be sold in due time at a higher price. We recommend the following guidelines for selling:

1. Sell when the price has advanced 50% or in two years, whichever comes first. We have adopted this guideline from Ben Graham's work and have observed for ourselves its validity. Also, one of David Dreman's studies shows the value for the two-year time frame.

2. Sell when the low P/E ratio rises to the P/E ratio for the market as a whole due to price appreciation or an earnings decline.

3. Sell when a company loses money or eliminates its dividend. Losses reduce the book value of the corporation and often signal deep problems. Unless you are a very experienced analyst and can make an in-dpeth analysis of the company's problems, loss companies as a rule should be avoided.

4. Another time to sell is when the stock being sold can be replaced by a much better bargain. For example, assume you're holding a B company when a C company becomes available at an attractive price. It would be advantageous, then, to sell the B company and trade up in quality.

Table 10-2. Annualized compound rates of return, May 1970–February 1973.

Stocks Ranked By P/E Multiples Decile	Switching After Each:				Holding Original Portfolio for 2¾ Years
	1 Quarter	6 Months	1 Year	2 Years	
1 (highest)	13.07%	12.51%	15.78%	12.84%	12.40%
2	19.19	20.66	15.05	12.04	13.01
3	14.11	15.49	17.64	16.17	15.86
4	13.95	13.27	14.34	13.12	14.97
5	10.71	10.56	12.66	13.32	16.94
6	13.19	15.88	15.75	12.22	12.98
7	14.83	14.26	13.10	15.39	16.01
8	15.06	14.54	14.19	16.93	17.23
9	16.45	17.93	17.56	19.36	14.20
10	20.35	16.09	15.41	18.56	15.28

Average return of sample. . . . . .14.54%.

Source: Dreman, *Contrarian Investment Strategy*, p. 134.

Conclusion

This chapter has presented the information necessary to actively manage port-folios of low P/E-ratio stocks. Be reminded that, if C companies are not available, you can put together a portfolio of B stocks that by definition will require a sell target, either time or price.

When companies meeting philosophy-B requirements are not available, because of valuation disparities that exist occasionally between stocks and bonds, you should invest in three- to five-year high-quality bonds, either treasuries or tax-exempt municipals, and wait until the next buying oppor-tunity. Making investments based on definable value is the key to success in the stock market.

APPENDIX A
GLOSSARY

Bottom-up approach. Centers on stock selection and selects those that are undervalued the most. Usually, value is based on forecast or perceived earnings power or asset value.

"Cash flow" per share. Net profit plus non-cash charges (depreciation, depletion, and amortization), less preferred dividends (if any), divided by common shares outstanding at year end.

Common equity. Net worth less the liquidating or redemption value of any preferred issues outstanding. Represents the sum of the value of common stock at par, the surplus of capital received (over par) from the sale of common stock (i.e., capital surplus), and retained earnings (i.e., earned surplus). Retained earnings here is the sum of net profits earned in all years less dividends paid in all years.

Common equity ratio. Common equity divided by total capital (i.e., long-term debt, preferred equity, and common equity).

Current assets. Assets that may reasonably be expected to be converted into cash, sold, or consumed during the normal operating cycle of the business, normally 12 months or less. Current assets include cash, U.S. Government bonds, receivables, and inventories.

Current dividend yield. The dividends that were paid by the company over the past 12 months as a percentage of the recent price.

Current liabilities. Liabilities that must be satisfied within the next 12 months. Current liabilities include trade accounts payable, taxes, wage accruals, current installments on long-term debt, and notes payable.

Current price-earnings (P/E) ratio. The recent price divided by the earnings reported by the company for the past 12 months.

Depreciation. The amount charged against operating profits in any one year to allow for the aging of plant and equipment owned by the company, plus depletion and amortization charged to operating income in a fiscal year. Accelerated-depreciation accounting (as opposed to the more common straight-line method) is considered conservative.

Depreciation rate. The total amount of depreciation, depletion, and amortization charged to income during the year, expressed as a percentage of gross plant (i.e., total plant and equipment including land at original cost as reported by the company) at year end.

Income tax rate. Federal, foreign, and state income taxes (including deferred taxes) reported to stockholders, divided by pre-tax income reported to stockholders. This is not the true tax rate shown in IRS tax filings; it is the "book tax rate" and measures earnings quality. As a rule of thumb, the lower the figure below the 45% to 48% range, the poorer the reported earnings quality.

Inventory turnover. Sales divided by year-end inventory.

Long-term debt. All debt due in more than 12 months.

Modern portfolio theory. Measures and defines the risk of a particular stock in relation to the market. It compares risk-adjusted performances of various portfolios and breaks a security's return into components showing that portion attributed to the market, beta, and that portion attributed to individual selection, alpha. This individual selection process identifies undervalued stocks in relation to their forecast value.

Net plant. Total plant and equipment, including land, at original cost as reported by the company, less accumulated reserves for depreciation.

Net profit. Sales less all expenses (including cost of goods, general and administrative expenses, depreciation, interest, and taxes). Net profit is before (i.e., excludes) "extraordinary" gains and losses, and to this extent differs from the net income figure reported by corporations in their financial statements. Net profit is after (i.e., includes) so-called after-tax "special" gains and losses (including as a rule items related to discontinued operations) and pre-tax "unusual" items.

Net worth. All the assets shown on the balance sheet including any intangible assets (i.e., goodwill, debt discount, deferred charges) *less* current liabilities, long-term debt, and all other noncurrent liabilities. In other words, the sum of common plus preferred stockholders' equity including intangibles.

Operating margin. Operating earnings (before deduction of depreciation, depletion, amortization, interest, and income tax) as a percentage of sales or revenues.

Payout ratio. The sum of all cash dividends (common and preferred) declared for the calendar or fiscal year divided by net profit for the year, and expressed as a percentage.

Percent earned common equity. Net profit less preferred dividends divided by common equity (i.e., net worth less preferred equity at liquidating or redemption value), and expressed as a percentage. (See **Percent earned total capital.**)

Percent earned net worth. Net profit divided by net worth, and expressed as a percentage. (See **Percent earned total capital.**)

Percent earned total capital. Net profit plus one half the interest charges on long-term debt, divided by total capital (i.e., long-term debt plus net worth), and expressed as a percentage. Measures the earning power of the company, assuming all capital is equity; should be compared to **Percent earned net worth** to determine impact of leverage (i.e., use of borrowed capital) to enhance the return of stockholders.

Percent retained to common equity. Net profits less all common and preferred dividends divided by common equity including intangible assets, and expressed as a percentage. Also known as the Plowback ratio.

Pretax margin. Profits before federal, state, and foreign income taxes as a percentage of sales or revenues.

Retained earnings. When relating to the income account, represents net profit for the year less all common and preferred dividends. With respect to the balance sheet or common equity, it is the sum of net profit in all years of the company's existence, less all dividends (common and preferred) ever paid. In this case, also known as earnings retained or earned surplus.

Sales. Gross volume less returns, discounts, and allowances, in other words, net sales.

Short-term debt. All debt due in the next 12 months and considered a current liability.

Tangible book value per share. Net worth less intangible assets and less preferred stock at liquidating or redemption value, divided by common shares outstanding at year end.

Technical analysis theory. The use of charts and other devices to aid the practitioner in forecasting future market and stock price moves.

Top-down approach. Begins with a forecast of the economy, then selects industries that should do well within that economic picture, and finally selects the best companies in those industries.

Total capital. The sum of long-term debt, preferred stock at liquidating or redemption value, and common equity including intangibles.

Total debt. The sum of long-term debt and short-term debt.

Working capital. Total current assets less total current liabilities. Working capital (or net current assets) includes such current assets as cash and governments, receivables, and inventories less such current liabilities as accounts payable, current taxes, dividends payable, short-term bank notes, and the portion of the long-term debt that comes due over the next 12 months.

Note: most of these definitions are from the *Value Line Investment Survey* glossary.

APPENDIX B: SUPPLEMENTAL READING LIST

For those readers who would like to learn more about value investing and some of the people who shaped our thoughts, we suggest the following books and articles.

Books

The Intelligent Investor by Benjamin Graham, 4th ed., New York: Harper & Row, 1973.

The Money Masters by John Train, New York: Harper & Row, 1980.

Contrarian Investment Strategy by David Dreman, New York: Random House, 1979.

Security Analysis by Benjamin Graham, David L. Dodd, and Sidney Cottle, 4th ed., New York: McGraw-Hill Book Company, 1962.

Supermoney by Adam Smith, New York: Random House, 1972, especially chapter 5, pp. 173-199.

Articles

"Ben Graham's Last Will and Testament," by Paul Blustein, *Forbes,* August 1, 1977, p. 43

"Remembering Benjamin Graham—Teacher and Friend," by James B. Rea, *The Journal of Portfolio Management,* Summer 1977, p. 66.

"How Inflation Swindles the Equity Investor," by Warren E. Buffett, *Fortune Magazine,* May 1977, p. 251.

"A Conversation with Benjamin Graham," by Charles D. Ellis, *Financial Analysts Journal* September-October, 1976.

"Ben Graham: Ideas as Mementos," by Charles D. Ellis, *Financial Analysts Journal,* July-August, 1982.

Annual Reports

Berkshire Hathaway, Inc., Annual Letters to Shareholders 1977-81. Write to Berkshire Hathaway, Inc., 1440 Kiewit Plaza, Omaha, NE 68131, or call (402) 346-1400 for a copy.

Other

Rea-Graham Fund information—Toll-free, Bank of New York (1-800) 221-2990, extension 8164, for a quote. Write Jim Rea, 10966 Chalon Road, Los Angeles, CA 90077, or phone (312) 471-1917 for the fund Prospectus or for information on the Graham-Rea Investment Analysis Screens.

The Value Line Investment Survey, 711 Third Avenue, New York, NY 10017, or call (212) 687-3965 for subscriber information.

The Standard & Poor's Compustat Services, Inc., Printed Products Dept., 7400 So. Alton Ct., Englewood, CO 80112, or call (303) 771-6510 for Financial Dynamics subscription information.

Kidder Peabody & Co., 10 Hanover Square, New York, NY 10005, (212) 747-2773 ask for Barre W. Littel or call your local Kidder Peabody & Co. broker. Barre W. Littel produces the FQP (Financial Quality Profile) which is the most accurate cash flow analysis available anywhere.

There are three funds one can look at:

Berkshire Hathaway—not a fund but a diversified company run by Warren Buffett.

Sequoia Fund—A fund run by William J. Ruane (a student of Graham and friend of Buffett) 1290 Avenue of the Americas, New York, NY 10104.

Source Capitol—A closed-end fund, run by George H. Michaelis. First Pacific Advisors, Inc., 10301 West Pico Boulevard, Los Angeles, CA 90064.

Questions or comments, write:
Skip Bowen and Frank Ganucheau
P.O. Box 910
Fort Worth, Texas 76101

Appendix C: Additional Research and Observation on the Low P/E Philosophy

Following is additional proof of the superior results obtained by applying the low P/E-ratio approach to equity management. Chapters 2 and 4 covered the major researchers and practitioners using this approach. This appendix presents other researchers who have written about low P/E-ratio investing.

This discussion of researchers and practitioners is divided into two groups, as it was in chapters 2 and 4. Group A, the original group of early researchers, consist of Henry S. Schneider, James D. McWilliams, and William Breen. Group B, the group of researchers who built on the theoretical framework of the people in Group A, consist of James B. Rea, Dr. J. Sanjoy Basu, Ernest R. Widmann, Steven C. Leuthold, Clinton M. Bidwell, and John R. Riddle.

Group A—Additions to the original group

Henry S. Schneider, researcher, student of Graham. Schneider also demonstrated the efficacy of the low P/E-ratio philosophy. Schneider, who worked at Wertheim & Co., wrote an article for the *Journal of Finance* in 1951, "Two Formula Methods for Choosing Common Stocks." He compared the period 1914 through 1948 and found an interesting pre-New Deal, post-New Deal occurrence. Tables C-1 and C-2 show the differences between the two period performances of low P/E-ratio, or "cheap-group" stock, versus high P/E-ratio, or "dear-group" stocks. Table C-3 shows the full time period, 1914 to 1948.

Table C-1. Pre-New Deal results (1914-1931): a total percentage pluses and minuses.

	One-Year Tests (18)	Two-Year Tests (18)	Three-Year Tests (18)
Cheap group:			
Total of plus years	+ 168	+ 464	+ 469
Total of minus years . . .	− 198	− 254	− 276
Grand total	− 30	+ 210	+ 193
Dear group:			
Total of plus years	+ 378	+ 507	+ 592
Total of minus years . . .	− 187	− 252	− 238
Grand total	+ 191	+ 255	+ 354
Dow Jones Industrial Avg.:			
Total of plus years	+ 244	+ 431	+ 487
Total of minus years . . .	− 173	− 221	− 227
Grand total	+ 71	+ 210	+ 260

Source: Henry S. Schneider, "Two Formula Methods for Choosing Common Stocks," *Journal of Finance,* June 1951, p. 230.

Table C-2. New Deal results (1932-48): a total percentage pluses and minuses.

	One Year Tests (17)	Two Year Tests (16)	Three Year Tests (15)
Cheap group:			
Total of plus years	+ 425	+ 570	+ 754
Total of minus years . . .	− 51	− 54	− 47
Grand total	+ 374	+ 516	+ 707
Dear group:			
Total of plus years	+ 250	+ 330	+ 406
Total of minus years . . .	− 90	− 129	− 134
Grand total	+ 160	+ 201	+ 272
Dow Jones Industrial Avg.:			
Total of plus years	+ 239	+ 335	+ 417
Total of minus years . . .	− 74	− 87	− 74
Grand total	+ 165	+ 248	+ 343

Source: Schneider, "Two Formula Methods," p. 231.

Table C-3. Summary of results (1914-48): a total percentage pluses and minuses.

	One-Year Tests (35)	Two-Year Tests (34)	Three-Year Tests (33)
Cheap group:			
Total of plus years	+ 593	+ 1,034	+ 1,223
Total of minus years . . .	− 249	− 308	− 323
Grand Total	+ 344	+ 726	+ 900
Dear group:			
Total of plus years	+ 628	+ 837	+ 998
Total of minus years . . .	− 277	− 381	− 372
Grand total	+ 351	+ 456	+ 626
Dow Jones Industrial Avg.:			
Total of plus years	+ 483	+ 766	+ 904
Total of minus years . . .	− 247	− 308	− 301
Grand total	+ 236	+ 458	+ 603

Source: Schneider, "Two Formula Methods," p. 232.

As can be seen in Table C-1, 1914-1931, the "Dear group" outperformed the other two groups. Contrarily, in the period 1932-48, Table C-2, the "Cheap group" outperformed the others by a wide margin, reaffirming the validity of the low P/E-ratio philosophy. When the two periods are taken as a whole, Table C-3, the low P/E-ratio philosophy again asserts itself in superior performance. But Schneider wanted to know why it did not happen in the 1914 to 1931 period. Schneider said:

> During 1914-31 the market was gradually establishing those wide quality-differentials which have been so prominent a feature of common stocks ever since the New Era bull market of the late 1920s. In 1914 the dividend yields and earnings multipliers for our large companies were rather homogeneous; but as time went on, the "good stocks"—meaning particularly those with favorable earnings trends—became valued more and more generously vis-a-vis the "lower quality" issues. This bias in favor of the quality issues was

an accelerating affair; its result was to favor the good stocks in the market year after year, even though they had already outperformed the rest of the list. This bias continued through the Great Depression culminating in 1932. In those years the quality issues appeared to justify the favor previously accorded them, because they showed better resistance to the hard times.

We suggest finally that the quality differentials had been fully established by 1932, so that the bias in favor of the good stocks was now completely reflected in their prices. From then on the basic element of fluctuation reasserted itself: good stocks, like good markets, went up too high; unpopular stocks, like unpopular markets, went down too far.

If our explanation is a sound one, we would conclude that the performance in the 1932-48 period is more likely to be duplicated in future years than that of 1914-31. Our method of selecting "cheap stocks"— or something similar thereto—might therefore prove to offer both an extremely simple and a reasonably dependable key to successful stock selection (Schneider, "Two Formula Methods," p. 233).

Studies to be cited later will confirm the validity of Schneider's conclusions regarding the differences between these two time periods.

James D. McWilliams: the computer Guru adds his firepower. McWilliams conducted a study using Standard & Poor's Compustat Industrial Tapes of 900 companies. McWilliams used the following criteria to select his companies.

1. A complete 12-year history of April 30 prices had to be available.
2. Only New York Stock Exchange and American Stock Exchange-listed companies were eligible; no over-the-counter companies.
3. Only companies with fiscal years ending on December 31 were eligible.

As a result of these qualifiers, McWilliams identified 390 companies to be included in the testing universe. The P/E ratios were calculated by dividing the April 30 price by earnings-per-share for the accounting year ending the prior December 31. Then McWilliams divided the 390 companies into deciles, or 10 groups, from low P/E-ratio stocks to high P/E-ratio stocks. The results again proved the efficacy of the low P/E-ratio approach. Table C-4 and Chart C-1 give the results. Chart C-1 shows the deciles compounded over the test period, which ran from the end of 1952 to the end of 1964.

Table C-4. Average returns of 390 stock sample by deciles for years ending April 30.

P-E Deciles	1964 %	1963 %	1962 %	1961 %	1960 %	1959 %	1958 %	1957 %	1956 %	1955 %	1954 %	1953 %	Average %
Low 1	20	12	15	28	2	64	−5	8	27	68	25	15	23
2	21	8	5	27	0	66	−9	4	25	77	11	24	22
3	21	12	2	28	−2	53	−4	6	21	61	10	15	18
4	22	9	3	24	−0	67	1	2	20	51	20	17	20
5	19	4	−2	28	−2	52	−3	1	24	49	12	9	16
6	12	2	−1	27	−4	39	−1	2	24	42	14	9	14
7	11	5	−1	23	1	51	2	8	19	43	21	12	16
8	17	5	−6	32	−4	43	−2	9	21	41	12	11	15
9	14	1	−6	29	−5	47	−2	3	31	35	10	9	14
High 10	27	7	−12	20	−4	65	−5	−1	28	43	10	8	15
Average	19	6	0	27	−1	55	−3	4	24	51	14	13	17

Source: James D. McWilliams, "Prices, Earnings, and P-E Ratios," *Financial Analysts Journal,* May-June 1966, p. 138.

Chart C-1. Results of investing $10,000 in different P-E deciles 1952-64.

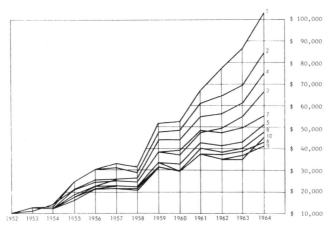

Source: McWilliams, "Prices, Earnings and P-E Ratios," p. 138.

For the 12-year test period, high P/E-ratio stocks outperformed low P/E-ratio stocks during three years and then by only 1% in 1956, 1% in 1959, and 7% in 1964. There was one tie in 1958. For the remaining years, the low P/E-ratio stocks outperformed the high P/E-ratio stocks by a wide margin.

McWilliams then studied the variability of the performance of stocks within each group. With low P/E-ratio stocks consistently outperforming high P/E-ratio stocks, McWilliams wondered if the best performers were in the low P/E-ratio group. As a result, he examined the facts and found that, for the most part, big winners could be found in any of the ten different P/E-ratio groups. This raised the question about why the low P/E-ratio stocks were outperforming the high P/E-ratio stocks.

McWilliams asked the reverse of the above question: In what decile were most of the poorest-performing stocks to be found? After close examination of the facts, McWilliams found that consistently fewer stocks declined in the low P/E-ratio groups, while the high P/E-ratio groups had an above-average number of declining stocks. In fact, the proportion of low P/E-ratio declining stocks to high P/E-ratio declining stocks was one to four. McWilliams states:

> Weaving the results of the extremely good and the extremely poor performers together in the analytical decision making process, it appears that we can find good performers anywhere but if you are looking at high P/E stocks, great care must be exercised to determine that the company in question is going to keep on growing. This is the area where it appears that the investor frequently bids multiples and prices up too sharply in relation to actual growth and the investor is subsequently disappointed (McWilliams, "Prices, Earnings and P-E Ratios," p. 142).

Interestingly enough, Miller and Widmann came to a similar conclusion independently of McWilliams.

At the time of this study, McWilliams was an Investment Officer in the Trust Department of the Continental Illinois National Bank in Chicago. He was in charge of computer approaches to analysis of common stocks and of portfolio selection for the bank.

William Breen, industry relatives. Breen, in an article entitled, "Low Price-Earnings Ratios and Industry Relatives," July-August 1968 *Financial Analysts Journal,* asks this question: Should a price-to-earnings ratio be considered low in relation to the *whole market,* or in relation to the *industry* in which the company is classified? Earlier, Nicholson touched on this issue when he conducted his studies on the chemical industry. But, since then, the issue had not been addressed.

Breen used the Compustat tapes of 1,800 industrial companies. His test period ran from 1952 through 1966. Breen screened the information and eliminated all companies that had less than a 10% growth in earnings over the past five years. Then he selected ten stocks for each of two portfolios each year. The first portfolio contained the ten lowest P/E ratio stocks in relation to the over-all market. The second portfolio contained the ten stocks that had the lowest P/E ratio in relation to their industry group (Table C-5). Another study was done using 50 stocks (Table C-6). Tables C-5 and C-6 show the results for the different portfolios.

Table C-5. Ten lowest P/E-ratio stocks related to over-all market (Portfolio One) and then to Industry Relatives (Portfolio Two).

Year/Return	Low Market Relatives	Low Industry Relatives
	Portfolio One	Portfolio Two
1953	0.1928 (95%)	0.1328 (95%)
1954	0.5751 (95%)	0.9248 (95%)
1955	0.4517 (95%)	0.3554 (95%)
1956	0.1940 (90%)	0.0769 (65%)
1957	−0.0986 (45%)	−0.1564 (20%)
1958	1.1159 (95%)	0.7263 (95%)
1959	1.0285 (95%)	0.6108 (95%)
1960	0.1370 (90%)	0.1212 (90%)
1961	1.5519 (95%)	0.3606 (70%)
1962	−0.0419 (95%)	−0.1982 (35%)
1963	0.2554 (75%)	0.3376 (90%)
1964	0.2610 (80%)	0.2672 (80%)
1965	0.5050 (80%)	0.2202 (15%)
1966	0.0343 (85%)	0.0608 (90%)
Mean compound return	0.375	0.239

Note: Number in parentheses is the percent of randomly chosen portfolios in that year that had returns less than or equal to the given return.

Source: William Breen, "Low Price-Earnings Ratios and Industry Relatives," *Financial Analysts Journal,* July-August 1968, p. 126.

Table C-6. Fifty lowest P/E-ratio stocks related to overall market (Portfolio One) and then to industry relatives (Portfolio Two).

Year/Return	Portfolio One	Portfolio Two
1953	0.0249	0.0347
1954	0.8897	0.9015
1955	0.3424	0.3247
1956	0.2160	0.1549
1957	− 0.1178	− 0.1949
1958	1.0230	0.8378
1959	0.6101	0.6088
1960	0.0502	0.1084
1961	0.7334	0.6633
1962	− 0.0903	− 0.1268
1963	0.3672	0.3708
1964	0.2756	0.2398
1965	0.5112	0.3741
1966	0.0048	− 0.0264
Mean compound return	0.301	0.263

Source: William Breen, "Low Price-Earnings Ratios," p. 127.

As can be seen, whether 10 stocks or 50 stocks were used in each portfolio, the results were essentially the same. That was ". . . returns from portfolio one are larger than returns from portfolio two, still indicating that the market-relative concept is superior to the industry-relative concept (Breen, p. 127). Therefore, according to Breen, there is no advantage to using an industry-relative P/E-ratio concept.

The market-relative concept worked better. Breen tried one more time, combining the ten lowest ratios of company P/E ratios to average industry P/E ratios that also were among the 50 lowest absolute price-to-earnings ratios. This provided a double screen, which, as shown in Table C-7, produced the same results. No appreciable difference was found. **Portfolio One in Table C-5 seems to dominate, proving the use of market relatives versus industry relatives.**

Table C-7. Ten lowest P/E-ratio stocks related to industry relatives which were also among 50 lowest overall market P/Es.

Year	Return	Percent of Random Less Than Return
1953	0.1298	(95)
1954	0.9264	(95)
1955	0.3554	(95)
1956	0.2274	(90)
1957	− 0.1695	(15)
1958	0.7480	(95)
1959	0.5611	(95)
1960	0.1443	(90)
1961	1.3842	(95)
1962	− 0.1832	(40)
1963	0.3466	(90)
1964	0.3027	(85)
1965	0.2621	(25)
1966	0.0866	(90)
Mean compound return	0.310	

Note (right column): Percent of randomly chosen portfolios in that year that had returns less than or equal to the given return.

Source: William Breen, "Low Price-Earnings Ratios," p. 127.

Group B—Additions to the contemporary researchers

James Buchanan Rea. Rea specialized in searching for undervalued corporations that could be candidates for acquisition by his clients. Through articles sent to him by clients, Rea became familiar with Graham's work. Rea arranged to meet with Graham to discuss mutual interests. Later they worked together, testing different valuation criteria. Eventually they established a fund that utilized their methods. There were ten criteria that today are fairly well established.

FIRST FIVE: PRICE SENSITIVE

1. The earnings yield is to be twice the average AAA bond yield. For example, if the AAA bond yield were 12%, twice that would be 24. This means the price-to-earnings ratio would be 4.2 or less.
2. The P/E ratio is to be no more than 40% of its previous average high.
3. The price of a particular stock is to be equal to or less than two thirds of its tangible book value.
4. The dividend yield is to be equal to or greater than two thirds of the average AAA bond yield.
5. The price is to be at or below the stock's "net current asset value."

SECOND FIVE: FINANCIAL STRENGTH AND EARNINGS

1. The ratio of current assets to current liabilities is to be two or higher.
2. The total debt is to be less than the company's tangible net worth. (The company should owe less than it is worth.)
3. The total debt is to be less than twice the current assets minus the sum of current liabilities, long-term debt, minority interest, deferred taxes, leasehold liabilities, pension liabilities, and preferred stock.
4. Rate of growth of earnings over the past ten years is to be at least 7% compounded annually.
5. There should be no more than two declines in year-end earnings, relative to the preceding year, in the past ten years.

The theoretical basis of Graham and Rea's work relates P/E ratios to bond yields. They related the cheapness of a stock to its P/E ratio and/or to its dividend yield. They established valuation criteria to define the expensiveness of a stock and the value the investor receives for his invested dollar. The results of their tests, using these criteria, are as follows: If the "earnings yield criterion," low P/E ratio, were the sole criterion, the performance would have been 19.9% compared to the Dow Jones performance of 7.5% from 1925 through 1975.[1]

As an additional check, some of Graham's and Rea's students at the graduate School of Management, University of California at Los Angeles, ran a ten-year study using all ten of their criteria. The results showed that by using the ten criteria they would have more than doubled the performance of the Dow-Jones Industrial Average. When Graham said they could use only two criteria and do as well, they ran the test again. The two criteria were (a) total debt less than equity and (b) earnings yield twice the average AAA bond yield or low P/E-ratio. The results, over the ten-year period, of a test run independently by graduate students at the University of California, Los Angeles, proved that a portfolio compiled by using these two criteria would have performed twice as well as the Dow Jones's performance (Rea, "Remembering Benjamin Graham," pp. 66-72).

Rea started a limited-partnership fund on June 30, 1976. It is now a full-fledged mutual fund called the Graham-Rea Fund. From June 30, 1976, through December 31, 1982, the fund produced a compound growth, after all costs, of 18.06% per year. The Dow-Jones averages during this period produced a compound growth of 6.3% per year. The Graham-Rea fund did 187% better than the Dow-Jones averages!

Sanjoy Basu, a genius in hiding! Basu was a professor at McMaster University in Hamilton, Canada. Basu has written two major articles on price-to-earnings ratios. They are,

> "The Information Content of Price Earnings Ratios, *Financial Management,* Summer 1975.

> "Investment Performance of Common Stocks in Relation to Their Price-Earnings Ratio: A Test of the Efficient Market Hypothesis," *Journal of Finance,* June 1977.

In these two related articles, Basu sets out to determine whether the investment performance of common stocks is related to their P/E ratios.

In the first article, Basu states his goals. He reaffirms them in the second article, using a somewhat different presentation:

> The price-earnings (P/E) ratio and dividend yield are probably the two most frequently used in the investment community. Theory and previous empirical research indicate that although a host of financial variables including risk, payout, and leverage account for differences in P/E ratios of corporate equities, the principal explanatory factor is the expectation of growth in earnings and dividends. While the precise manner in which these expectations are formed by the market is unclear, historical growth rates, recent earnings and other corporate announcements, and market forecasts at the economy-wide and industry levels are believed to be significant. Capital market efficiency implies that all such information is fully impounded in security prices in a rapid and unbiased fashion. While an impressive body of empirical evidence supports the efficient markets hypothesis, there does exist some evidence to the contrary. In particular, studies

by Breen & Savage, Breen, McWilliams, Miller & Widmann, and Nicholson challenge market efficiency in processing information implicit in price-earnings ratios. These studies suggest that P/E ratios may be indicators of future investment performance of securities. However, these studies have significant shortcomings that include retroactive selection bias, i.e., sample being composed of only 'survived' firms and the failure to account for risk differentials, portfolio related costs, e.g., transactions costs, and differential tax effects.

This article attempts to overcome these limitations. It presents the results of empirical examination of the market's reaction in the months following the announcement of annual income reports to securities trading at different multiples of earnings. Specifically, the intention is to ascertain whether securities with different price-earnings ratios are 'appropriately priced' vis-à-vis one another, or whether certain groups yield 'abnormal' returns. In other words, does the market capitalize earnings of firms in an unbiased manner? (Basu, "The Information Content," p. 53.)

Basu began his study by performing primary research on individual stock performance, using the P/E ratio, and covering a period from 1956 through August of 1971.

His data base and criteria for selection of firms were as follows.

1. The Compustat file of New York Stock Exchange industrial firms, the related Investment Return file from the Compustat tape, and a delisted file containing selected accounting data and investment returns for securities delisted from the New York Stock Exchange were used. With the inclusion of the delisted file, 375 to 400 firms, the group represents over 1,400 industrial firms which actually traded on the New York Stock Exchange between September 1956 and August 1971.
2. The fiscal year-end of the firm had to be December 31. The fiscal years are 1956 through 1969.
3. The stock must have traded on the New York Stock Exchange as of the beginning of the holding period for the portfolio.
4. The relevant investment return and financial statement data must be available.

From this selection came a total of 753 companies satisfying the criteria for at least one year. About 500 of these 753 companies satisfied all the criteria for all 14 years.

The price-to-earnings ratios were calculated, using year-end earnings and prices. Obviously, these were not available until later, so on April 1, when 90% of the earnings had been reported, the P/E ratios were calculated for year end, using year-end prices and reported year-end earnings. Then the companies were ranked by P/E ratio, and five groups were formed with about 100 companies in each group. The procedure was repeated for each year of the study. Table C-8 shows the results, as adapted from Basu's original table.

Table C-8. Performance of stocks according to P/E ranking (April 1957–March 1971).

P/E Quintile	Median P/E Ratio	Yearly Compound Growth	Beta or Systematic Risk	Jensen's Measure or Differential Return
A	35.8x	9.3%	1.11	− 3.3
A*	30.5x	9.6%	1.06	− 2.6
B	19.1x	9.3%	1.04	− 2.8
C	15.0x	11.7%	0.97	0.2
D	12.8x	13.6%	0.94	2.3
E	9.8x	16.3%	0.99	4.7

A*—Excludes firms with negative earnings.

Source: Basu, "Investment Performance of Common Stocks," p. 667.

The low P/E ratio portfolios, D and E, earned 13.6% and 16.3% per annum, respectively, over the 14-year period. Contrarily, the high P/E-ratio portfolios, A, A*, and B, earned 9.3%, 9.6%, and 9.3% per annum, respectively, over the 14-year period. There is no doubt that this is a significant difference. In fact, the lower the P/E ratio, the better the return.

Another major point of the study was to disprove the notion that the lower P/E-ratio stocks and higher returns were associated with high risk measured by beta. Each group's beta, risk, was calculated and noted on the table. The results show that beta, risk, declines as P/E multiples decline. This is in spite of the higher returns and challenges the "capital market theory" idea that higher returns must be associated with higher beta, risk.

Basu also evaluates the differential return, or Jensen's measure, a statistical test, on the different groups. This shows that the high P/E-ratio group earned

2.8% to 3.3% *less* than an associated random portfolio of equivalent risk, while the low P/E-ratio groups earned 2.3% to 4.7% *more* than an associated random portfolio of equivalent risk.

Basu's studies accomplished three things:

1. His highly sophisticated, statistical approach to handling the data eliminated any of the early arguments on methodology.
2. He added proof to the effectiveness of the low P/E-ratio approach to stock selection through his studies, as shown in Table C-8.
3. He proved that the increased return from low P/E-ratio stocks is *not* associated with increased risk, beta, as the "capital market theory" would lead one to believe.

In conclusion, the behavior of security prices over the 14-year period studied is, perhaps, not completely described by the efficient market hypothesis. To the extent low P/E portfolios did earn superior returns on a risk-adjusted basis, the propositions of the price-ratio hypothesis on the securities and their P/E ratios seem to be valid. Contrary to the growing belief that publicly available information is instantaneously impounded in security prices, there seem to be lags and frictions in the adjustment process. As a result, publicly available P/E ratios seem to possess "information content" and may warrant an investor's attention at the time of portfolio formation or revision (Basu, "Investment Performance," pp. 680-681).

Ernest R. Widmann: early work with Paul Miller leads to low P/E ratio and high yield. Addressing the investment community, especially the employee benefit tax-free fund managers, Ernest R. Widmann wrote a position paper in August 1974 called "High Compound Investing: An Alternative to Growth Stock Investing." This paper emphasized the income portion of total return. In the process of searching for high-yield stocks, without buying utility company stocks, Widmann directed his portfolio toward low P/E-ratio stocks.

Widmann was fully conscious of this phenomenon because he had worked with Paul Miller on the low P/E-ratio approach in the mid-'60s. Widmann, however, chose to present and market the concept in a different manner. His first studies used the Dow Jones Industrial Averages. Later studies used the Standard & Poor's 400 averages, a larger universe for more statistical significance.

In the Dow Jones study, Widmann, as previously with Miller, divided the Dow stocks by three groups. The groups were the low-yield group, the high-yield group, and all 30 Dow stocks. The difference in this study was that they were separated by current-yield versus price-to-earnings ratios. Table C-9 summarizes the results.

	30 D.J.I.A. Stocks	Ten Low Yield D.J.I.A. Stocks	Ten High Yield D.J.I.A. Stocks
1954-78	9.4%	7.1%	12.7%

Table C-9. Performance — annual rate of return.

Source: Ernest R. Widmann, "Does Yield on Stocks Still Matter?" in *Total Return Overview,* Widmann, Blee & Co., Philadelphia, May 1979, p. 2.

High-yield or low P/E-ratio stocks again showed superior results. Widmann then used the Standard & Poor's 400 to test the philosophy. He took the 400 list and divided it into five groups, or quintiles, each group having 80 stocks. Table C-10 shows the results.

Table C-10. Performance — annual rate of return.

	S&P 80 High Yield Stocks	S&P 80 Low Yield Stocks	S&P 400 Stocks
1973-81	15.5%	11.2%	11.1%

Source: Ernest R. Widmann, "High Yield Group Top Performers in 1981," in *Total Return Overview,* Widmann, Blee & Co., Philadelphia, February 1982, pp. 2-3.

Again, the results are impressive. High-yield stocks, or low P/E-ratio stocks, do not outperform low-yield stocks, or high P/E-ratio stocks every year. But, over the years, the results from the studies seem to be fairly conclusive.

Steven C. Leuthold, bottom fishing. Leuthold, President of the Leuthold Group, has done extensive work on stock market subgroups. The purpose of Leuthold's studies is to group stocks into microgroups, then to track them fundamentally and technically. Through this work, Leuthold has come to the conclusion that, "Market success often comes from buying stocks that are out of vogue."[2] . . . This usually means low P/E ratios. Leuthold has one "concept group" he calls the "undervalued and unloved." He states the following rationale and criteria:

Rationale

These are the real cheapies. There is no fundamental or economic commonalty built into this screen, nor is "growth" a factor. This concept combines quality and value considerations only. *To qualify for this grouping, a stock must satisfy six of the seven criteria below.* We also arbitrarily eliminated all non-telephone utilities.[3]

Leuthold's criteria are,

(1.) Book Value Ratio must be less than 80% of the Standard & Poor's 500 Book Value ratio. (2.) P/E Ratio based on 5-year average earnings must be less than 70% of the Standard & Poor's 500 P/E Ratio. (3.) The Ratio of Cash per Share to Price per Share must be at least 15%. (4.) The Indicated Dividend Yield must be at least as high as the Standard & Poor's 500 Yield. (5.) The Ratio of Long-Term Debt plus Unfunded Pension Liabilities to Total Capital must be less than 50%. (6.) The Cash Flow Ratio must be less than 75% of the Standard & Poor's 500 Cash Flow Ratio. (Company stock price to company cash flow per share compared to S&P 500 price to cash flow per share.) (7.) Financial Strength must be above average (Leuthold, p. 41).

These criteria quickly eliminate high P/E-ratio companies or high price-to-book-value companies.

Over the past eight years, the performance resulting from the use of these criteria has been good.

Chart C-2.

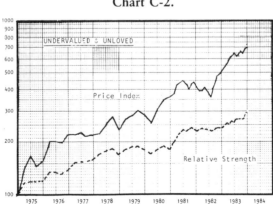

Leuthold is not a pure low P/E-ratio exponent. For example, he has a section called "the intriguers." This presents criteria based on technical factors only, where Leuthold attempts to find groups of stocks that have performed poorly and are showing signs of technical improvement. When this happens, the stocks go on the "intriguers" list. Leuthold's objective is to cross-reference the "undervalued and unloved" with the "intriguers" and arrive at a common list of stocks.

The method does not have a long enough track record to prove itself. However, the "undervalued and unloved" group, which consists of low P/E-ratio stocks as well as low price-to-book value stocks with above average financial strength, does have a performance record better than the general market averages.

Clinton M. Bidwell, III, and John R. Riddle: opportunities for profits. Bidwell and Riddle have written an article entitled "Market Inefficiencies — Opportunities for Profits" that appeared in *Journal of Accounting Auditing and Finance,* Spring 1981.[4]

Bidwell and Riddle used P/E-ratio calculations and "standardized unexpected earnings" as two mechanical criteria. For our purposes, we are interested only in the P/E-ratio study. The study was conducted for nine quarters and involved 853 to 917 companies in any quarter. The period ran from the third quarter of 1976 through the third quarter of 1978. Bidwell and Riddle's conclusions on P/E ratios were that the low P/E-ratio portfolio *outperformed* both the high P/E-ratio portfolios as well as the sample populations in each of the nine test periods.

References

1. James B. Rea, "Remembering Benjamin Graham—Teacher and Friend," *The Journal of Portfolio Management,* Summer 1977, pp. 66-72.
2. Charles J. Ella, "Bottom Fishing For Out-of-Favor Stocks Seen as Good Strategy by Developer of a Technique," *Heard on the Street, Wall Street Journal,* December 1976.
3. Steven C. Leuthold, "Undervalued & Unloved," *Perception: For The Professional,* November 1982, p. 41.
4. Clinton M. Bidwell III, and John R. Riddle, "Market Inefficiencies—Opportunities For Profits," *Journal of Accounting Auditing & Finance,* Spring 1981, pp. 198-214.

APPENDIX D: PRICE VS. REINVESTMENT RATE: WHICH IS THE MORE IMPORTANT VARIABLE?

The focus of this book has been on how an investor can have his wealth compound through common stock ownership. The case has been made that:

1. If the company has good economic characteristics, and
2. The stock is acquired at the right price, the owners of the business will prosper as the business prospers and will earn approximately the rate of return on their investment that the corporation earns on its invested capital (over the long run). Often investors seek out companies with high growth and high return on equity and rationalize paying high prices to own them because of their visible growth prospects. We, again, take the other side of the argument. We will show why price is a more important consideration than the reinvestment rate. Two examples using the Investor's Equation will demonstrate the fallacies of paying too much for growth.

	Company A	Company B
Return on equity	14%	18%
Earnings per share	$7	$9
Market price and book value	$50/50	$108/50
Price earnings ratio	7.14x	12x
Dividend	$2.10	$1.80
Yield	4.2%	1.6%
Internal reinvestment rate . . .	9.8%	14.4%
Total return	14%	16%
(Yield + reinvestment rate)		

In its simplest form, the Investor's Equation treats the earnings yield as an annuity that compounds at the total return rate. By using a business calculator, one can compute that Company A will double the investor's wealth in 5.29 years, while Company B will double the investor's wealth in 7.22 years (assuming the market-price-to-book-value ratios remain the same).

Company A. $.14 received each year growing at 14% equals $1.00 in 5.29 years, i.e., the same period a 14% coupon bond will double, assuming the income stream is reinvested at 14%.

Company B. $.083 received each year growing at 16% equals $1.00 in 7.23 years, i.e., the same period a 10.05% coupon bond will double, assuming the income stream is reinvested at 10.05%.

Even though Company B has a higher return on equity and a lower payout ratio, its high price makes it a less-attractive investment than Company A. Price is the most important variable of the two.

APPENDIX E
COMPOUND INTEREST TABLES

This section contains two standard compound interest tables, denominated in terms of $1, that will be very useful in implementing the philosophy advocated in this book. Here is a brief explanation (and example) on how to use the table.

The first table, Present Worth to Future Worth, shows the amount to which one dollar will grow at a given rate of compound interest over a stated number of time periods. For example, if $200 is deposited in a 12% C.D., how much will it be worth in six years? $200 × 1.974 = $394.80.

The second table is Annuity to Future Worth, based on the assumption that for each period a payment is made of one dollar and left to compound at the stated interest rate. For example, assume $100 is deposited yearly in a C.D. growing at 12%. How much will the fund be worth in five years? $100 × 6.353 = $635.30.

We developed the Investor's Equation to have a method of relating the compounding effect of bonds to stocks. In its simplest form, it treats the earnings yield of the stock as an annuity and compounds this sum at the total return for the stock. The time period it takes for this amount to equal 100 is the payback period. By looking at a compound interest table, the investor can use this payback period to calculate the coupon rate equivalent for a bond investment. For example, assume a stock has a P/E ratio of 8 and a total return (internal reinvestment rate plus yield) of 16%, what would be its payback period? Earnings yield: $\frac{1}{8} = 12.5 \times 6.877 = 85.96 < 100$

$$\frac{1}{8} = 12.5 \times 8.977 = 112.21 > 100.$$

By trial-and-error multiplication of the factors under the 16% column on the annuity table (6.9877 and 8.977), we arrive at the conclusion that five years is too short and six years is too long. The annuity of 12.5 growing at 16% will equal 100 in approximately 5.5 years. By looking at the table of Present Worth to Future Worth, the investor can determine the rate required to have money double in 5.5 years. Under the 14% column: $1 = $1.925 in five years and $2.195 in six years. Consequently, money approximately doubles in five and one-half years at 14%, so the stock in the example is roughly equivalent to a 14% coupon bond.

Present Worth to Future Worth (Compound Sum of $1)

Year n	8%	9%	10%	12%	14%	15%	16%
1	1.080	1.090	1.100	1.120	1.140	1.150	1.160
2	1.166	1.188	1.210	1.254	1.300	1.322	1.346
3	1.260	1.295	1.331	1.405	1.482	1.521	1.561
4	1.360	1.412	1.464	1.574	1.689	1.749	1.811
5	1.469	1.539	1.611	1.762	1.925	2.011	2.100
6	1.587	1.677	1.772	1.974	2.195	2.313	2.436
7	1.714	1.828	1.949	2.211	2.502	2.660	2.826
8	1.851	1.993	2.144	2.476	2.853	3.059	3.278
9	1.999	2.172	2.385	2.773	3.252	3.518	3.803
10	2.159	2.367	2.594	3.106	3.707	4.046	4.411
11	2.332	2.580	2.853	3.479	4.226	4.652	5.117
12	2.518	2.813	3.138	3.896	4.818	5.350	5.936
13	2.720	3.066	3.452	4.363	5.492	6.153	6.886
14	2.937	3.342	3.797	4.887	6.261	7.076	7.988
15	3.172	3.642	4.177	5.474	7.138	8.137	9.266
16	3.426	3.970	4.595	6.130	8.137	9.358	10.748
17	3.700	4.328	5.054	6.866	9.276	10.761	12.468
18	3.996	4.717	5.560	7.690	10.575	12.375	14.463
19	4.316	5.142	6.116	8.613	12.056	14.232	16.777
20	4.661	5.604	6.728	9.646	13.743	16.367	19.461
25	6.848	8.623	10.835	17.000	26.462	32.919	40.874

Annuity to Future Worth

Year n	8%	9%	10%	12%	14%	16%	18%
1	1.000	1.000	1.100	1.100	1.000	1.000	1.000
2	2.080	2.090	2.100	2.120	2.140	2.160	2.180
3	3.246	3.278	3.310	3.374	3.440	3.506	3.572
4	4.506	4.573	4.641	4.770	4.921	5.066	5.215
5	5.867	5.985	6.105	6.353	6.610	6.877	7.154
6	7.336	7.523	7.716	8.115	8.536	8.977	9.442
7	8.923	9.200	9.487	10.089	10.730	11.414	12.142
8	10.637	11.028	11.436	12.300	13.233	14.240	15.327
9	12.488	13.021	13.579	14.776	16.085	17.518	19.086
10	14.487	15.193	15.937	17.549	19.337	21.321	23.521
11	16.645	17.560	18.531	20.655	23.044	25.733	28.755
12	18.977	20.141	21.384	24.133	27.271	30.850	34.931
13	21.495	22.953	24.523	28.029	32.089	36.786	42.219
14	24.215	26.019	27.975	32.393	37.581	43.672	50.818
15	27.152	29.361	31.772	37.280	43.842	51.660	60.965
16	30.324	33.003	35.950	42.753	50.980	60.925	72.939
17	33.750	36.974	40.545	48.884	59.118	71.673	87.068
18	37.450	41.301	45.599	55.750	68.394	84.141	103.740
19	41.446	46.018	51.159	63.440	78.969	98.603	123.414
20	45.762	52.160	57.275	72.052	91.025	115.380	146.628
25	73.106	84.701	98.347	133.334	181.871	249.214	342.603

BIBLIOGRAPHY

American Telephone & Telegraph Company, *Annual Report,* 1982, 1981, 1980.

Babcock, Guilford C. "The Concept of Sustainable Growth." *Financial Analysts Journal,* May-June 1970.

Basu, Sanjoy. "The Information Content of Price-Earnings Ratios." *Financial Management,* Summer 1975.

——————. "Investment Performance of Common Stocks in Relation to their Price-Earnings Ratio: A Test of the Efficient Market Hypothesis." *The Journal of Finance,* June 1977.

Bernhard, Arnold. "Investing in Common Stocks." *Value Line Investment Survey,* 1975.

Bernstein, Leopold A. *Financial Statement Analysis: Theory Application and Interpretation.* The Willard J. Graham Series in Accounting. Rev. ed. 1978. Consulting ed. Robert N. Anthony. Homewood, Ill.: Richard D. Irwin, 1978.

Bidwell, Clinton M. III and Riddle, John R. "Market Inefficiencies — Opportunities for Profits." *Journal of Accounting Auditing & Finance,* Spring 1981.

Block, Frank E. "The Place of Book Value in Common Stock Evaluation." *Financial Analysts Journal,* March-April 1964.

Brealy, Richard. *An Introduction To Risk and Return From Common Stocks.* Cambridge, Mass.: M.I.T. Press, 1969.

Breen, William. "Low Price-Earnings Ratios and Industry Relatives." *Financial Analysts Journal,* July-August 1968.

Buffett, Warren E. "How Inflation Swindles the Equity Investor." *Fortune Magazine,* May 1977.

Capaldi, Benedict E. Jr. "Low P/Es: Optimal investing: The Stage is currently being set for a recovery of these stocks. *Pension & Investments Age,* December 1982.

Christy, George A. and Roden, Peyton Foster. *Finance: Environment and Decisions.* 2nd ed. New York: Canfield Press, 1976.

Dow Chemical Company, *Annual Report* (1982).

Dreman, David. *Contrarian Investment Strategy: The Psychology of Stock Market Success.* New York: Random House, 1979.

Drucker, Peter F. "Measuring Business Performance." *Wall Street Journal,* August 3, 1976.

Ella, Charles J. "Bottom Fishing for Out-of-Favor Stocks Seen As Good Strategy by Developer of a Technique." *Heard on the Street, Wall Street Journal,* December 3, 1976.

Ellis, Charles D. "A Conversation With Benjamin Graham." *Financial Analysts Journal,* September-October 1976.

——————. "Ben Graham: Ideas as Mementos." *Financial Analysts Journal,* July-August 1982.

——————. "The Losers Game." *Financial Analysts Journal,* July-August 1975.

Fama, Eugene F. "The Behavior of Stock Market Prices." *Journal of Business,* January 1965.

"Firms Turn to Basics in Slack Bond Market," *Pension & Investment Age,* February 20, 1984.

Fuller, Russell and Petry, Glenn H. "Inflation, Return on Equity and Stock Prices." *Journal of Portfolio Management,* Summer 1981.

Graham, Benjamin; Dodd, David L.; and Cottle, Sidney. *Security Analysis: Principles and Technique,* 4th ed. New York: McGraw-Hill, 1962.

——————. *The Intelligent Investor: A Book of Practical Counsel.* 3rd ed. New York: Harper & Brothers, 1959.

——————. *The Intelligent Investor: A Book of Practical Counsel.* 4th ed. New York: Harper & Row, 1973.

Greenbaum, Mary. "Gauging the Market's Prospects." *Fortune,* Time, Inc., January 10, 1983.

Greene, Richard. "Are More Chryslers in the Offing?" *Forbes,* February 2, 1981.

Hawkins, David F. "Inflation, Market Efficiency and Accounting Data: Keys to Identifying the Corporate and Investor Winners." *Accounting Bulletin 3, Drexel Burnham & Company,* May 1974.

Hersch, Otis and O'Conner, William P. Jr. "Quality Measurement of Stocks." *The Fourteen Research Corporation,* 1982.

Hitschler, Anthony W. "Strategy Results from December 1958 through December 1978 Using Total Sample." *Provident Capital Management Inc.* Private unpublished study. Used by permission.

——————. "To Know What We Don't Know or the Caribou Weren't in the Estimates." *Financial Analysts Journal,* January-February 1980.

Homer, Sidney and Liebowitz, Martin L. *Inside The Yield Book: New Tools For Bond Market Strategy.* Englewood Cliffs, N.J.: Prentice-Hall, 1972; New York: New York Institute of Finance, 1972.

"How the Forecasters Went Wrong in 1981." *Business Week,* December 28, 1981.

Ibbotson, Roger G. and Sinquefield, Rex A. *Stocks, Bonds, Bills and Inflation: The Past and the Future.* 1982 ed.

International Harvester Company, *Notice of Special Meeting of Stockholders,* October 28, 1982.

Largay, James A. III and Stickney, Clyde P. "Cash Flows, Ratio Analysis and the W. T. Grant Company Bankruptcy." *Financial Analysts Journal,* July-August 1980.

Leuthold, Steven C. "Undervalued & Unloved." *Perceptions: For the Professional,* November 1982.

Littel, Barre W. CFA and Levine, Robert. "Financial Quality Profile—Introduction to FQP Theory, Ratios and Scoring." *Kidder, Peabody, & Company,* December 19, 1980.

Lorie, James H. and Hamilton, Mary T. *The Stock Market: Theories and Evidence.* Homewood, Ill.: Richard D. Irwin, 1973.

McWilliams, James D. "Price, Earnings and P-E Ratios." *Financial Analysts Journal,* May-June 1966.

Miller, Paul F. "Drexel & Co. Monthly Review." *Drexel & Co.,* October 1966.

Miller, Paul F. and Widmann, Ernest R. "Price Performance Outlook for High & Low P/E Stocks." *Commercial and Financial Chronicle, 1966 Stock and Bond Issue,* September 29, 1966.

Molodovsky, Nicholas. "Recent Studies of P/E Ratios." *Financial Analysts Journal,* May-June 1967.

"Moody's Bond Record." *Moody's Investors Services, Inc.* March, 1984.

Nicholson, Francis S. "Price-Earnings Ratios." *Financial Analysts Journal,* July-August 1960.

——————. "Price Ratios in Relation to Investment Results." *Financial Analysts Journal,* January-February 1968.

Peavy, John W. III and Goodman, David A. "The Interaction of Firm Size and Price-Earnings Ratios on Portfolio Performance." *Edwin L. Cox School of Business, Southern Methodist University,* March 1983.

——————. "The Significance of P/Es for Portfolio Returns." *Journal of Portfolio Management,* Winter 1983.

Porter, Michael E. *Competitive Strategy: Techniques for Analyzing Industries and Competitors.* New York: Free Press, 1980.

——————. "Industry Structure and Competitive Strategy: Keys to Profitability." *Financial Analysts Journal* July-August 1980.

Dictionary of the English Language: Unabridged Ed. New York: Random House, 1973.

Rea, James B. "Remembering Benjamin Graham—Teacher and Friend." *Journal of Portfolio Management,* Summer 1977.

Reilly, Frank K. *Investment Analysis and Portfolio Management.* Hinsdale, Ill.: Dryden Press, 1979.

R. J. Reynolds Industries, Inc. *Annual Report,* 1982.

Salomon Jr., R. S., "Financial Assets—Return to Favor," *Salomon Brothers Inc. Investment Policy,* June 10, 1983.

Schneider, Henry S., "Two Formula Methods for Choosing Common Stocks." *Journal of Finance,* June 1951.

"Selection & Opinion." *The Value Line Investment Survey,* February 25, 1983, 1977 and 1981.

Sharpe, William F. Evolution of Modern Portfolio Theory." *C.F.A. Readings in Financial Analysis* 5th ed., Institute of Chartered Financial Analysts. Homewood Ill., Richard D. Irwin, 1981.

——————. "Likely Gains from Market Timing," *Financial Analysts Journal,* March-April 1975.

Standard & Poor's Compustat Services, Inc., Financial Dynamics Industrials, "Annual Financial Analysis," (Various Company sheets).

——————. Standard & Poor's Compustat Services, Inc., *Financial Dynamics Standard & Poor's 400 Industrial Composite, 1981, 1982, 1983.*

Train, John. *Dance of the Money Bees: A Professional Speaks Frankly on Investing.* New York: Harper & Row, 1974.

——————. *The Money Masters.* New York: Harper & Row, 1980.

Union Carbide Corporation Annual Report. (1982)

Value Line Incorporated, *Value Line Investment Survey,* "Ratings & Reports," (various company sheets).

Value Line Inc., Selections & Opinions, *Value Line 900 Industrial Composite,* July 1983 & 1978.

Widmann, Ernest R. "Does Yield on Stocks Still Matter?" *Total Return Overview Widmann, Blee & Co.* May 1979.

——————. "High Yield Group Top Performers in 1981." *Total Return Overview Widmann, Blee & Co.,* February 1982.

INDEX